INSIDE GAME

THE TRUE STORY OF
THE NBA BETTING SCANDAL

HOW TEMPTATION TURNED A GOOD GUY BAD AND HIS STORY OF REDEMPTION

THOMAS MARTINO

This is the true story of the NBA scandal based on the experience and from the perspective of Thomas Martino one of the 3 defendants in the case.

With the exception of brief quotations in review-with proper accreditation-no part of this ebook may be used, reproduced, or transmitted in any manner whatsoever without written permission from the author

Limits of Liability/Disclaimer of warranty:

The authors and publishers of this eBook and the accompanying materials have used their best efforts in preparing this book. The authors and publishers make no representation or warranties with respect to the accuracy, applicability, fitness, or completeness of the contents of this book. They disclaim any warranties (expressed or implied), merchantability, or fitness for any particular purpose.

The authors and publishers shall in no event be held liable for any loss or other damages, including, but not limited to, special, incidental, consequential, or other damages.

As always, the advice of a competent legal, tax, accounting, or other professional should be sought. This book contains material protected under International and Federal Copyright Laws and Treaties. Any unauthorized reprint or use of this material is prohibited.

This book is for educational purposes only.

Published by Phillybomber Publishing

©Copyright 2019

ISBN: 9781692360153

Book Design by Ellen Violette & The Book Business Abundance Team
Book Editing by Ellen Violette

"Each of us involved in the NBA betting scandal has our own story to share, and Thomas Martino shares his brilliantly in *Inside Game.* From JP Morgan, to driver for a mob-connected gambler, to convicted felon, Thomas leaves no stone unturned. It's heart wrenching and raw and I promise you won't be able to put it down. Bravo Tommy!"

Tim Donaghy
Former NBA Referee

Dedication

I'm dedicating this book to my wife Ashley and my 3-year-old son Thomas Francis. I'm twenty years older than Ashley and fifty years older than Thomas. They will be here long after I'm gone, and I don't want them holding the bag. The only bag I want them holding is one of gold so that they don't have to worry about a thing when I'm gone. It was my son, my wife and God who gave me the strength and will power to finish this book. My goal is to prepare my family for life without me. And that is my legacy!

The greatest gift is a portion of thyself.
Ralph Waldo Emerson.

Go to the back of the book to claim your free private interview," Easy Money til It Wasn't" video, with author, Thomas Martino, only available with purchase of this book.

Table of Contents

Foreword

My name is Scott Wolf. I am an actor and producer. You may remember me from my roles in Party of Five (1994), White Squall (1996), and Night Shift (2014). My latest project is Inside Game.

I've been lucky to be part of telling some great stories over the course of my career, on and off camera. But none have been more fun to tell than this one, the true events behind the 2007 NBA Betting Scandal, told from the perspective of one of the central figures, Tommy Martino.

I had the good fortune of playing Tommy. Before we started filming, I got to spend time with him, and I found him to be genuine and intelligent. He readily admitted he was not free from blame, but he also wanted the world to know he is not the culprit depicted by the press. It was important to Tommy that the story be told truthfully, out of respect to those who lived through it.

I liked Tommy right away. He's charming, funny, lives squarely in each moment, and is game for a good time, anytime. It's easy to see how he could be persuaded to join in this caper with two of his oldest friends, Jimmy Battista and NBA referee Tim Donaghy, to jump into the deep end even if he wasn't sure there was water in the pool since he's the kind of guy who jumps first and asks questions later.

Unfortunately for Tommy, "later" came just a few months into the scheme, when the FBI arrested him. Tommy went from being a respected IT specialist, employed by a reputable banking firm, to an unemployed felon with a damaged reputation.

Although his role was tangential, Tommy suffered the same punishment as the others involved in the case. He survived months of investigation, six months in the notorious MDC prison in Brooklyn, and another half year in a prison camp outside Boston. He emerged to write a gripping book describing the ordeal.

What follows here is the personal, behind-the-scenes story of one of the biggest sports-betting scandals in history - how it all began, how it took flight, how it all came crashing down, and finally, the price paid. I can say unequivocally that the book is a true representation of events. It is sometimes brutally frank, at other times poignant, but always honest and exciting.

I can't say I think everything Tommy and his friends did was smart, or right, or good. But having played Tommy on screen, I can say that I get why it seemed like a great idea at the time, and as Tommy says at the end of the film, they've got a hell of a story to tell. This is that story.

CHAPTER 1

Growing Up Martino

I am from the suburbs of Philadelphia; therefore, I am a Philadelphian. I wouldn't want to live anywhere else. I still live where I was born and raised-in an area called Delaware County or as us "townies" prefer to say, Delco. Delco is known for its gamblers, bookmakers, mobsters, wanna-be mobsters, rednecks, motorcycle groups and NBA referees. Some people who aren't from Delco refer to us as a cult, but if they were born and raised here, they would call it home just like I do.

As a first -grader at Westbrook Park Elementary School, in Springfield, I started experimenting with everything interesting and non-interesting that came about during any given day. One hot summer day, I remember coming face to face with bird shit staring back at me from an awning pole. The next thing I knew I was tasting it … and I had this out of body experience. I felt drunk for a second for the first time in my life. I ended up catching myself before I fell backwards off the railing and onto my ass. It was not one of my best decisions; something I'll never forget and never do again. What was it about my nature that made me taste the bird shit? I'm not sure, but I think it could help explain my penchant for risk taking.

I mention this because for forty-six years, it is something that has stuck in my mind. When Thomas Francis turns six (an age which I consider appropriate for inappropriate story sharing), I'm going to relay this tale and make sure he doesn't experiment with bird shit, NBA referees and most importantly mobsters.

Prior to the bird-shit experiment, to a time when my brain starting functioning normally, or abnormally, depending on how you look at it, I can remember constantly asking myself and wondering, "What the fuck is going on around me? Why am I here? And where am I really?" I felt like half the stuff I was doing and being asked to do was bullshit … as it turns out I was right. But I was just a kid, and these were adults around me. Seasoned adults with good jobs and the authority to order me around.

So, I kept my mouth shut, kept my ideas to myself and went through the motions. I played *rope-a- dope* for the next thirty- some-odd years and, to this day, still wonder why we are all here. I didn't do well in school as a result of this incessant cerebral meandering. I was meant for bigger things. I needed to make a name for myself, and I didn't care to what lengths I had to go to do it. While teachers were teaching, I was thinking of other things. Their mouths were moving, but I heard not a single syllable.

I still remember my science teacher scolding me for saying, "If a tree falls in the forest with no one around it, it DOES make a noise". He insisted I was wrong and made me look like a damn fool in front of everyone, especially the cute little blonde girl in the front of the class I had my eye on. He was aware of this as he saw us walking the halls together and made sure he embarrassed me. I remember his response vividly, "Martino, "How could it make a noise if there is no human being there to hear it? A human ear must be present for the tree to make a noise."

I never told him because I was afraid of the impending humiliation that he would heap on me. I couldn't help but think, "What a horse's ass! Doesn't this moron realize there are animals in the forest that heard the tree fall? What if I put a tape recorder in that forest where the tree fell? Would it tape the sound the tree made?" There I was in a Catholic school, and my teacher was telling me the tree didn't make a noise because no one was present to hear it? Did he forget about GOD?

In religion class, just two hours prior, our priest told us that God hears and sees everything. To this day, that science teacher remains anonymous. He may be taller but I'll be the bigger man here. Even more now, I'm wondering,

"What the hell's going on?" I hated being in his classroom and prayed I wouldn't get him next year. But as fate would have it, I did. He must have had a say in it. I'm 100% sure. Any chance this man had to embarrass me in front of this girl, he did. It wasn't relegated to the classroom either.

The "Science Guy" threw verbal jabs in the cafeteria and at recess. Two places he couldn't harass me were on the football field and basketball court where I excelled and found peace, happiness and tranquility. I hope this never happens to my son because if it does, there will be hell to pay!

I'm writing this to give you an idea of my years before, during and after the scandal. I also want the world to know what really happened in the three months during which we rewrote the book on influencing professional sports. I'm going to stop short of saying fixing because there is a fine line between fixing and influencing. The question of fixing is for Tim Donaghy only, and in my eyes, if he were fixing he would have won all the games he gave us. Tim told me he could influence a game six points either way. Take that as you wish, that's what he told me.

This is a true account of my role in the scandal, and my dealings with Tim Donaghy and James (Babba) Battista. To this day, we remain friends. Enough time has passed and plenty of water has gone under the bridge for fences to mend. But I can assure you that's not going to stop me from telling my side of the story. It's a story of trust, betrayal, drugs, lust and above all, **GREED**. A desire that ultimately led to our downfall. The downfall of a plan that was to make us all millionaires. A perfect plan that was destined to fail much like all perfect plans. I'm writing not to glorify myself. but to share what really happened from my perspective. I don't know what Tim Donaghy or Jimmy Battista did when I wasn't around, but I will tell you what I know as I witnessed it.

Let me tell you a little bit about myself, I'm 5' 5" tall and 160 pounds. At my fighting weight, I was 117 pounds in high school. I dropped to 127 after spending thirty spine-chilling days in the hole in MDC Brooklyn, which I will get into further when I discuss in detail my incarceration. I say fighting weight because being a small guy made me a prime target for bullies. (A short stature was just cause for bullying in my early years.) It was around this time that I established myself as a fighter.

I recorded my first "W" right around first grade in the schoolyard at Westbrook Park Elementary School. We agreed to meet at the monkey bars and, of course, it was over the prettiest girl in the school. He was perceived to be the toughest kid in school because he looked the part. He thought if he beat me up, then he would win her affection. It was a Popeye/Bluto scenario for six-year-olds. The fight ended as quickly as it began.

I remember how everything went in slow motion as he charged at me like the Tasmanian devil; unleashing haymakers that only Bugs

Bunny could appreciate. So many thoughts ran through my mind, but I had no time to be afraid. Needless to say, I won the fight by TKO in twenty seconds of the first round and established myself as a force to be reckoned with. It took just one punch and, at that moment, one thing was for sure, I could fight!

My father always told me and my brothers don't ever start a fight and, most importantly, don't ever back down. Maybe that's why I won them all. It's easier to win a fight you don't start. Maybe God is watching. Maybe God likes the underdog. That was my motto growing up. I hated fighting. Every fight I was ever in I was forced into. I never want to hurt anyone, EVER! Unless, of course, you're trying to hurt me, my family or my friends. Unfortunately, I was in many fights due to the way of the world, and the fact that I would never back down. I'm not proud of my accomplishments in the schoolyards and the streets, but I want to give you an idea of how I fought my way through life! Every day, I fight!

I learned a lot from my dad and still do to this day-way more than I learned in any school I ever attended. Sometimes, you run into people who have wisdom beyond their years. Fortunately for me, I had to look no further than my father. Dear old dad! Boy, did I hit the jackpot. The real Rock of Gibraltar. If I could be half the man my dad is, I would consider myself a success. I know exactly how to raise my son; I'll just do what my dad did. If it weren't for my father, I'd be living on crates in South Philly somewhere.

My mom was a stay at home mom who raised three kids, each a year apart. We are considered Irish triplets. I know what it's like to have one child, I can't imagine the difficulties with three. I have no idea how the hell she did it! Good job, Mom! I likened her to a lioness protecting her three little cubs. We were a middle-class God-fearing family of five who loved unconditionally. We were that house where all the neighborhood kids would want to gather. There should have been a small Statue of Liberty on the front steps with a sign that read, "Give us your poor, your hungry but, most especially, your outcasts"! The Martinos treated everyone as if they were our own, with a particular affinity for the downtrodden. As my cousin, Paulie Martino, always says, "That's how we roll Tommy, that's how we roll".

Much of our family's success can be attributed to my grandfather Charles J. Martino. I just called him, Pop. He was a hardworking second-generation Italian who only went to the fourth grade. They used to hide him in trash cans from the truant officers because he was supposed to be in school. Pop used to scrounge for money by working his balls off at any odd job a fourth grader was qualified for. His father came over on the boat from Italy and had no job, so the kids had to work to make ends meet and to put food on the table.

Born in 1909, and faced with hardcore economic hardship associated with the Great Depression, Pop knew he had to work, and school was not an option. He was one of sixteen children who made thirteen dollars a week working to feed his family. The term used to describe the family was "the working poor". Pop wore different-sized shoes on his feet that were hand-me-downs and always too small. He was a workhorse who paved the way for future Martinos, including myself and Thomas Jr. His work ethic was passed down through generations of Martino men. No one can ever say that any Martino is lazy!

We all work hard, and family comes first! That's why when Timmy, Jimmy and I initially lawyered up, the first of my three attorneys, strategically appointed to me by Battista's lawyer, Jack McMahon, gave me the option of witness protection. I remember him vividly telling me how the FBI could relocate me to Florida in exchange for my confession. He hinted to the fact that the Gambino crime family was heavily involved and, if I decided to come clean, I would never see my family again.

My attorney also mentioned that the Feds were up his ass calling every day pleading with him to "get Martino to Brooklyn to spill his guts" and that time was running out. My balls hit the floor with a thump. I thought, "No fucking way will I be torn away from my family." I was scared shitless. I now believe this was a tactic by McMahon and Battista to make sure I didn't say a word. I changed lawyers a week later after becoming entangled in a perjury trap before a grand jury in Brooklyn. When you get pinched you think that lying is the way out. Looking back, a grand jury only asks questions they know the answers to...more on that later. Like I said, family comes first so I wasn't about to relocate.

Pop worked four jobs, and his hard work paid off. He saved and saved, so his kids and grandkids wouldn't have to endure what he did. A strong work ethic and a firm moral standing birthed his success and served him well in the United States Coast Guard. He finished his diverse career as a prison guard at Broad Meadows in Thornton, Pa. Broad Meadows is a county prison featured in the 2009 movie *Law Abiding Citizen*. He was a true warrior, short in stature (pictured on the next page). He was the epitome of what my Dad always told me (He lived up to the old adage my dad always told me): "Good things happen to good people just slowly. " Instead, I chose the fast track and got my wings clipped in the process. My grandfather was a ballbuster and any chance he got to bust my chops he took. Pop hated when I would leave my sports equipment on the lawn overnight. He would tell me all the time, "Tommy I'm warning you, your basketball is going to get stolen." I never listened. We eventually moved to Springfield, the town just blocks away. I changed schools and enrolled in Holy Cross the local Catholic school where I played organized basketball for the first time in my life.

I figured that in Springfield no one would steal my basketball or baseball glove, or even my football for that matter, so why bring them in? I'm just going to get them out the next day. The same mindset that often got me grounded for not making my bed. I mean, in Springfield, we used to sleep with the front door open with screens in the storm door, so we could catch the breeze on warm summer nights. It was safe then and still is to this day.

Without warning, my basketball vanished, so I got a new one and that one vanished too. Day after day, pieces of my athletic equipment went missing. Baseball gloves, nerf footballs, one by one, all stolen. Pop was right, and I was about to get my ass chewed out. He said, "I told you if you leave your stuff out somebody's going to steal it." For someone who only completed four levels of schooling, he was quite the prophet. There was a thief in the Mr. Rogers neighborhood, and I couldn't believe it. Of course, my spoiled Italian ass complained until my dad replaced the items. To my credit, I stopped leaving them outside and, with that, the thievery ceased.

Years later, my pop passed away. It sucked when Pop died, and I had to help my dad clean out his house, which sucked even more. I wasn't about to let Dad do it himself. It's a chore that no son wants to do. So, by design, I went with him that day. I walked by the chair where Pop used to bounce me off his knee; strolled through the kitchen paid witness to me scarfing down Mom Mom's (Mom Mom is what we called my grandmother who was Pops wife) gravy sandwiches. I finally made it to the basement, and I couldn't believe my eyes; there they lie, all the sports equipment that was stolen right from under my nose. Years of memories right there, staring back at me like a thief in the night.

My baseball gloves that took years to break in, my favorite basketballs with all the tread still intact, Christmas presents, birthday gifts...it was like a time machine. I didn't know whether to laugh or cry, so I did both. I felt like he was there with me, which he was. I even spoke to him that morning and thanked him for the lesson he taught me. I cracked the cold case. I finally uncovered the thief. To my amazement and delight, it was Pop. It made one of the most horrible days in my life more bearable.

It was at Holy Cross where I first met Jimmy Battista, and it was at this time my brother Johnny aptly named him Babba. He was the same age as Johnny, one year older than me, but I hung out with the older guys as well because myself and one other kid were the only two seventh-graders to start for the varsity football team. Basketball was another story. I was cut from the team in seventh grade because ultimately, it was evident, I just wasn't good enough. I'm not going to sit here and say that I got robbed and should have made the team. I pretty much sucked. But now I was obsessed with making the team. My Dad bought me a portable basketball court and, for the next year, I practiced my ass off twenty-four hours a day, even in my sleep. I made the team the following year and started.

By season's end, I was one of the best players on the court and went to the all-star game with my good friend John Downey. Practice does make perfect, and I'm a prime example. Now don't get me wrong, Allen Iverson is one of my favorite Sixers of all time, but when he said the famous "We-talkin'-bout-practice" rant, I had to disagree because I know firsthand what practice did for me. More than likely, Iverson would have made five more shots a game had he attended practice.

Disclaimer: To all you kids out there who want to be better, you must practice or else get used to pulling splinters out of your ass during the game. Not too long ago, at a benefit for a close friend of mine, one of my former coaches, John (Pudgy) Geary, approached me with a beer in hand and said, "Tommy, you were the greatest player I ever coached." The sentiment was very genuine. It was from the heart, not the liquid in the red cup. The impression I got from the look on his face was that he wanted to tell me this for a while. I got choked up that day as it was one of the greatest compliments anyone has ever paid me.

There's been many a great player who scorched the hardwood floors at Holy Cross gym. I didn't say it that night, and it has haunted me ever since. Now that I have the platform, I want to say that Pudgie, John, was by far the best coach I ever had! And that's a terrific class of great coaches. To mention a few: Jack Rayer, the legendary Tom Flaherty, Frankie Long, Dan Butler, Danny Cardell, Bill McCusker, Brian Fox and dear old dad. But the moral to this story is to the kids who want to be better, you can do it, just practice!

"People see things as they are and say why?
I dream of things that never were and say why not?"
Bobby Kennedy

CHAPTER 2

The Unusual Suspects

In an effort to make it easier for you, the reader, and to better understand the upcoming chapters, I'm going to list the band of characters that I dealt with and a brief description of each.

Tim "Elvis" Donaghy: Veteran NBA Referee and close friend who provided me with NBA picks, which I, in turn, conveyed to James Battista, confidential informant.

James "Babba" Battista: Professional Gambler and close, childhood friend to whom I relayed Donaghy's picks.

Jack Concannon: Suburban Philadelphia Insurance Salesman and friend of Tim Donaghy who in 2003 allegedly partnered with Donaghy and Pete Ruggieri to bet on games, which Donaghy refereed. Another alleged confidential informant who was never charged with any crime.

Pete Ruggieri: Professional Gambler and occasional partner of James Battista who took over the scheme when Battista entered rehab. Also, an alleged confidential informant for the FBI who also was never charged with any crime.

Phil Scala: FBI Agent and Head of the Investigative Unit focused on the Gambino crime family at the time of the NBA scandal who mostly dealt with Tim Donaghy.

Taylor "Popeye" Breton: Gambler, Bookmaker, "money mover" and, as it turns out, the alleged source of the leak that ultimately led to the FBI uncovering the scandal.

The SHU: Special Housing Unit; affectionately referred to as "The Hole" in MDC Brooklyn. They should have called it the shit hole. Special housing unit my ass!

Water world: The Kitchen in MDC Brooklyn where I worked. Aptly named because workers get soaked from head to toe. They should have called it the end of the world. It was here that you had to slide your feet on the floor in order to walk. If you took steps, your ass would wind up flat on the floor. The floors were so slippery and repulsive that you could get a staph infection just looking at them.

Larry Crites: Six-foot Six-inch Leg Breaker from Taunton, Massachusetts and my personal bodyguard at MDC Brooklyn. He continues to be my bodyguard to this day. Critesy was a proud member of my wedding party.

"Schmogga": Term used by Tim Donaghy to alert me of a mortal lock.

The Chinaman: One of the best handicappers in the world.

Danny Malatesta: Childhood friend to the present day who served time in Fort Dix for bookmaking and loan sharking, pictured on the next page to the right of me in the tank top and my buddy, Spike, to the left.

Paul Harris and Jerry Conrad: FBI Agents assigned to break my balls.

Vicki Herr: Attorney and personal friend who did a phenomenal job defending me. She paid special attention to details of the case that ultimately led to a reduced sentence. She truly put everything she had into the case.

Eddie Portella: Prison Pal and fellow inmate at Fort Devens who fixed inmate's credit scores from jail. He also kept me well fed and entertained. If I could hang out with one person from Fort Devens today, it would be Eddie. I really miss him!

CHAPTER 3

From JP Morgan Chase to a Living Hell

I would be remiss if I didn't mention that I spent nineteen years of my life working in the IT department as a computer technician at JPMorgan Chase. I started in the print pool making $6.50 an hour back in February 1988 until the summer of July 2007, when my face hit the front page of the NY Post, and I was escorted out at twelve noon. I remember being led out that terrible day and thinking, as I made my way through the parking lot to my car, that I would never return. I have nothing but fond memories of my years at JPMorgan as I owe a lot to the company. I bought the house I still live in and many sports cars, including one of two Lotus models I owned while working there. They happen to be my favorite. Like myself, they pack a wallop in a very small package.

I snatched up an orange Lotus Elise once it hit American soil and a beautiful white 2006 Lotus Exige pictured on the next page. The accompanying vanity plate (MARTINO), that I still own, was a must. It now resides on my current car- an Alfa Romeo Quadrofolio. I miss my days at JPMorgan. They were an extension of my family. I played left field for the softball team (pictured on the page after the Lotus) and every position for flag football. I mean hell, it paid my bills, and I mastered my craft there.

I could fix anything related to a computer whether it was software, hardware, a printer or anything remotely or externally attached. They would send me everywhere to fix things others had failed to fix. I wouldn't leave until the job was done and done right. My skills have diminished a bit but I can still hold my own. Technology advanced and I didn't. I was too busy trying to save my life. With the investigation taking forever, jail, the halfway house and three- years' probation, you're looking at close to ten years of rebuilding. Suffice it to say, it's easier to repair a motherboard than the mess that was about to be my life. Not to mention, the new laws pertaining to full disclosure of felonies I faced following prison limited my options.My greatest asset was the art of dealing with the client. My brother, Johnny, calls me a chameleon. I could talk to anyone; adapt to any environment. I wasn't afraid of the big shots either. My brother was right; I mean if being a reptile every once in a while, translates into a raise next year, then color me a chameleon. It was devastating losing my job of nineteen years. A six-digit salary in 2007 was nothing to sneeze at. I knew how to play the corporate game: fly under the radar and be the only passenger on the plane. I would refuse promotions to higher positions like Officer and Vice President so that I could keep my overtime.

The higher-ups wanted to give me a three-thousand-dollar raise and take away fifteen- thousand in overtime. I don't think so! I watched show-offs with the big egos accept the title and forego the overtime but I'm not everyone else. I wasn't out for the prestige of a title. I was there to make as much money as I could so I could pay for my house and get any car I wanted. That was my goal. I ended up an officer of the bank, which was an elite accomplishment. To me, it's only a pat on the head they give you when you reach a certain pay grade.

JPMorgan allowed me to pay for my first wedding that incidentally was a royal wedding that I rushed into but don't regret. I learned from it. My father pulled me aside after my divorce and said the following, "Tommy, next time choose wisely my son." He got that from Indiana Jones, and I listened to him. I had to pay my now ex-wife a large sum of money and the furniture in exchange for freedom and the house! You can't put a price tag on peace of mind.

Divorcing the money was difficult too but worth every penny! She was a hard worker and a wonderful person. We just weren't the right fit, and I'm sure I had a lot to do with that. I was always better solo; duets just weren't my thing. I know she's happy now, and I'm happy for her. Everyone deserves to be happy, and that includes me and whoever might be reading this.

I have many fond memories in the two decades I worked at JPMorgan Chase but one in particular stands out, and I want to share it with you before I proceed with the chapters dealing with the scandal, my incarceration and the aftermath. Out of the blue, JPMorgan Chase decided to run an Easter-themed picture competition during the holiday month. I know it sounds a little strange but I do know for a fact that the person who invented this contest was also a participant. In other words, he had a picture he loved and wanted to show it off. If I recall correctly, he had just gotten back from vacation and was deeply into photography. Let's just call him Ron for shits and giggles because I forget his name. The prize? Two extra vacation days for the upcoming year to whomever had the most interesting picture associated with the holiday.

I remember seeing all these pictures outside the cafeteria pinned to a corkboard and I thought, not a single picture has anything to do with Easter. It was at that moment I realized I had the competition won. In my junk drawer at home, I had the best picture- one that would run away with the contest. Hands Down. No competition. I just had to go home and find it.

I had one more day to enter my picture. The cutoff was the next day, and I found it! It was a picture of my neighbor and good buddy, Joey Ferrigno, with Bunny Ears on top of his head. Joey was not only a friend of mine but a brother. Please know that he put the holiday ears on and posed in the picture on the next page.

Joey was one of the guys and we all treated him that way. He was in my wedding party and gave the best man speech. He brought the house down. We hung out each night and watched every Flyers game religiously. Never missed one. He was always at my side, and everyone loved him.

One day, a neighbor of ours stopped me in the street and said, "Tommy Martino! Oh my GOD! You are a saint! What you do for Joey is nothing short of amazing. You make his life worth living." It was very nice of her but I never really looked at it that way. I mean really, I did what I did because it's what we are supposed to do. I thanked her, and she went on her way. I never forgot that day and what she said. I think about it all the time because I no longer see Joey. Circumstances have created a chasm between the two of us.

I cherish the days and years we spent together. The truth is the joy I brought to Joey's life doesn't compare to the joy he brought me. It saddens me to think I'll never see him again; he was and still is one of a kind. He brightened up everyone's day-no matter where he was or who he was around. He was a diamond in the rough, and I was blessed to have him in my life.

But I digress...I entered the picture in the contest the morning of the due date and figured it was a lock. Well, I figured wrong. Donaghy must have been counting the ballots because after one week I sat in third place. With one week remaining, I needed a John-Elway-type comeback. I was losing...and I hate to lose. I remember one instance when my tennis partner, who I beat regularly, said after a defeat, "You can't win 'em all." I thought to myself, who says you can't win 'em all? I don't want this dude on my team. Ever! Incidentally, the owner of the picture currently in first place was Ron, the amateur photographer/creator of the competition. Talk about the fix being in.

Out of all the pictures entered, his related the least to the holiday. How in the hell was he beating me? Second place wasn't an option, especially if the ballots were being compromised. They had to have been; his picture sucked. It was of a pasture somewhere out in no man's land. It didn't make sense but he was a kiss ass, so I know he was going around soliciting votes. I overheard him one day bragging about his winning photo. He was gloating which made it worse, but I had an idea.

My picture clearly should have won the contest by a landslide. That being said, I took matters into my own hands. To prevent employees from voting more than once, each computer could only cast one ballot. If you attempted a second vote, it got rejected. Being in desktop support and a computer technician for the firm, I set up a dummy computer on the other side of the campus in a closet that no one could enter. Luckily, there was a network connection present. It took me about two hours, but I figured out how to vote as many times as I wanted. It was as simple as clearing out the cookies after every vote. I was elated!

I must have voted 500 times that day, and they had no way of knowing it was me. I went from third place to first in one day and ran away with the competition. I collected my extra two days of vacation and tacked it onto my six weeks. I won and that's what mattered. It was good to be the champion! The photographer sought me out to congratulate me on the victory but was acting goofy in the process. I guess he thought he had it in the bag. Kissing ass doesn't always pay off.

I can go on all day about the fun times at JPMorgan Chase. I used to take a bite from a donut and put it back in the box because I needed to lose weight, but I had to satisfy my sweet tooth. That must have pissed everyone off, especially the person that brought in the donuts. I always picked the juiciest one. I had to make it worth the calorie intake. That abruptly ended that fateful day in July 2007. I was having what the desktop group called "cocktail hour." This ritual consisted of five buddies drinking soft drinks around the breakroom table just outside the snack bar.

My buddy, Bill Walsh, rushed out from his office with the newspaper and screamed, "Tom, will you sign this? Can I have your autograph?" There it was, my face on the front page. Everybody's dream come true had become my worst nightmare. It finally hit the newspapers. The Feds were ready to prosecute and had more than enough evidence to come after us. My pager went off; Human resources was summoning me; people who once treated me nicely were now treating me like a gangster, a criminal. Word spread like wildfire that I was led out in handcuffs...dead man walking. I wasn't actually cuffed, but it was a long walk to the car. No more paychecks, no more health insurance, no more JPMorgan! Off to purgatory, I went!

"Great things don't last forever, that's what makes them great!"
Thomas Martino

CHAPTER 4

The Skunk in the Foxhole

Pete Ruggieri, with his children in tow, stepped out of his car in front of JPMorgan Chase one early spring afternoon after taking over for Jimmy Battista. He walked towards me, opened the sliding SUV door so I can see his beautiful children and said, "Jimmy took the winning lottery ticket, ripped it up and threw it out the window", his arm extended in a throwing motion. That pretty much summed it up. It was at that moment that I realized the depth of trouble we had gotten ourselves into. The hair on my arms stood straight up like the American flag being raised for the National Anthem. They were matched only by the chills racing down my back like a locomotive.

Pete had just taken over for Babba after his family whisked him away to rehab. It was my first dealing with Pete, and, at that time, I wasn't aware of this sensitive information. Evidently, Pete knew more than he was letting on. He also hinted to the fact that there were whispers about a group of low-level mobsters having an NBA referee in their hip pocket. I thought, "Holy shit, I hope to God they were just whispers." I don't want to get ahead of myself. I want to start from the beginning. Here goes!

James "Babba" Battista resurfaced after a long hiatus. He called me and asked if he could use my house to conduct some business-his alleged legal business of professional gambling. I believed this to be true. As P.T. Barnum famously proclaimed, "There's a sucker born every minute!" I didn't know what else he was up to, and as far as I was concerned, it was none of my business. He told me he was renting a room in a Valley Forge Hotel every day in the event his house got raided. This way his kids wouldn't have to endure the nightmare. That should have been a red flag right there, but I was happy to hear from him, and since I was recently divorced, I could sure use the company. I mean an escort here, a one-night stand there and an outbreak of shit-bird girlfriends only serves as a temporary plug to the dam.

He said he was being followed wherever he went. When he walked his dog at the park, getting coffee at Wawa, even getting his daughter off the bus. I didn't believe him. I thought he was trying to glorify himself as if being followed by the Feds was something to feel proud of. I always liked Jimmy, and I thought this could be a way to rekindle our childhood friendship. He offered me one-hundred dollars per day to conduct his business from my kitchen. I didn't just see dollar signs, I saw images of super cars flashing before my eyes. Yahtzee!

The interview was over; I hired Babba on the spot. His starting date was the next day as far as I was concerned. After all, it was kind of like an interview. He was feeling me out, and like the rest of Delco, Babba knows I'm a softy for someone in need, especially an old friend. Truth be told, our friendship never went away; it was just suspended for a while . To this day, we are still friends and just spoke the other day. I made him aware of the book I'm writing and he wished me all the success in the world. In the following chapters I will attempt to give you a depiction of how things went down on a molecular level.

Once the interview with Babba ended, I immediately had a key to my front door made at Home Depot. The following day, I handed it to Battista, and so the scandal began. He showed up to my home with a laptop and an array of burner phones. I believe the total was five. He would pace the kitchen floor watching sports channels on the big screen while fielding calls from every single phone. Placing bets, and, at times, (months later when things got hairy), arguing with the Chinaman about which side of the bet to be on. You shouldn't argue over a game with the best handicapper in the world. I thought that was strange. I'm sure it was a result of the drug abuse, but I only cared about passing GO and collecting my $100.

Don't get me wrong, I don't want to paint Babba as a drug addict. He wasn't always the hot mess he turned into, but I'm sure circumstances pushed him toward ingesting opioids and the White Devil, cocaine. Between the drugs and the stress of the betting, he would pace the floor he was like a caged animal walking back and forth and back and forth in my kitchen. I remember it like it was yesterday. I knew this wouldn't turn out well, but I was enjoying the action-and action is an understatement.

Babba had access to the wise guys and the top handicappers who had the best information on the NFL games and who was going to win on any given Sunday. My friends, including Donaghy, knew this, so every Sunday morning my phone would blow up with my friends asking what the plays were going to be. And whenever Donaghy called, he'd refer to Babba as "Beluga", as in whale, not only because of his rotund figure but because Babba had tried to recruit him earlier in his career when he was trying so hard to stay on the straight and narrow. Incidentally, I was his supplier; I'm partly to blame. I was supporting his downward spiral. It's crazy how a mind can justify any means to an end when the almighty dollar is involved. However, I was also unaware of what was going on behind the scenes. He asked me for cocaine, so I went and found a coke dealer, it wasn't difficult. The next phase of his addiction involved pills. This was a royal pain in the ass. There were never enough. He had an insatiable appetite for prescription opioids. The supplier is usually an asshole-bunch-of-shit-rip-off-artist because they got you by the balls.

I remember I would get ninety Vicodin a month from a girl at the gym who had a prescription. It was an easy get. They were blue. I paid top dollar, but so did Jimmy. It didn't matter the price, and money wasn't an issue, yet. The Vicodin wasn't enough, so I found another person with yellow banana Percocet tens. Skinny yellow-looking pills that looked appetizing, but being a recreational marijuana smoker, I wouldn't know.

One time, I took a half of a perc five at Babba's house. I ended up spending the night there with my friend La La. I got sick and shivered like a chihuahua. The room spun around and around, and it was hard not to throw up. There was no way I could get off the bed, let alone drive home. I felt like I had just gotten off the Gravitron-a ride at the carnival where you stick to the wall as it spins in circles while the guy next to you throws up right in his own face. I get sick just looking at that ride.

I got Babba anything he wanted me to get him. When he needed a rest from the opioids, I got him Suboxone. It wasn't like he was stopping, just a pit stop to recharge his battery. Every day, he would ask me for another bag of blow, easily an eight ball a day, which converts to three-and-a-half grams, which is the equivalent of an eighth of marijuana; that's why they call it eight ball; it's an eighth of an ounce.

One afternoon, I got home early and met my house cleaner as he exited my home. It was my cousin Brian, so there's never an awkward moment. I paid him the fee and asked how things went. His response literally "floored" me. He said, "Great, Tommy! I just did a line of coke off your kitchen tiles." Every once in a while, Babba would sneeze right before he did a line and blow it across the room. It didn't matter, I'd just go get another one.

We had a lot of fun and had each other's backs. We bonded. There were extravagant dinners with our significant others, and Babba always paid and over-tipped the wait staff, not to mention that he over-ordered from the menu. If the bill was $750 dollars, Babba would tip $750. One night, he bought drinks for the entire bar. This is something everyone has done before, but he went even further. Babba told the bartender to get everyone in the kitchen a drink from the head chef to the dishwasher. It was hilarious.

On another occasion, we were at the bar at a restaurant in Wayne Pennsylvania and the bill for the two of us was sixty dollars. Babba left a hundred-dollar bill as the tip. As we walked to the car, the wait-ress came running in our direction, waving the $100 bill. "Excuse me, sir! You left this on the bar!" she exclaimed. With that, we bent over in laughter and said, "Miss, you did a wonderful job, that hundred is for you!"

Babba was very generous and still is. He had plenty of cash that allowed him to be that way. He bailed out many a bettor who may have been in deep to local bookmakers. Those local bookmakers were "coincidentally" in deep to Babba. Friends would come to me and ask if I'd help them with a gambling debt. I told them only if you stop betting. This way, they wouldn't ask me again. I'd then ask for the bookmaker's name and forward the info to Babba. If he knew them, which he always did, since Delco is a haven for bookmakers, he would nod his head and say, "Hang on". One phone call later, the debt would disappear. I'm sure every bookmaker owed him, so he would say take it off my tab. He helped a lot of people.

One of his gifts to me was Flyers season tickets. I guarantee some degenerate gambler at Ticketmaster was indebted to Babba and bartered the seats for amnesty. I also got tickets to every sold-out concert event I wanted anywhere in the world. I even got tickets two-rows back for the Spice Girls 3 days before the event, which was next to impossible. No shit man, I mean life was a playground, and I was a 3-year-old. If I wanted Yankees tickets at Yankee Stadium, they would be at the box office waiting for me. My buddy, Peter, from Massachusetts, asked me for Celtics tickets- all he had to do was show up at the arena. The seats weren't in the boondocks either. I know mine were right on the ice or courtside.

I remember collecting money at the airport terminals in Philly from some dude, I forget his name; he allegedly worked for Ticketmaster. I'd pull up, and he'd hand me a stack of money while people were checking in for their flights. It was all in a day's work. I knew I'd be paid handsomely...in greenbacks or backstage passes.

One day, at Delaware Park, where the horses run, I was sitting outside waiting for the next race. Next to me was a beautiful Puerto-Rican girl from Rhode Island. I met her at a hair convention in Philly and flew her into town the following week. My phone rang and it was Babba. He asked if I was still at the race track. I told him yes and inquired as to why. He instructed me to put every dime I had on the four horse at Pimlico in the third race. I had about five dimes in my pocket, but I wasn't about to load up on this horse. It was a long shot at twenty-to-one odds.

I put $500 on it, and it ran away with the race post to post. I won ten-grand-plus my $500 back. He did this to me twice, and both times I chickened out with the amount I bet. I was a conservative and still am to this day: not a chicken, just a conservative. A lot of shit was going on; it felt like a movie. Things were out of control but nowhere near the level we were about to encounter in the months ahead.

"Here on earth, God's work must truly be our own."
JFK

CHAPTER 5

Unorganized Crime

There are many renditions of what transpired during that meeting in Philly. I was in the middle of it all and can now finally give my version of events. All three of us are very bright in our own way. Whether it be street smarts or common sense but, trust me, never book smart. None of us excelled in the classroom except for Tim on his SAT'S, that someone else took. But that's a story for another time. I like to refer to us as smart idiots, and we were about to agree to a deal with the devil-a one-way ticket to hell.

That day, during all his drug use, Battista called me on my cell phone, and in a serious voice told me we had to talk...in person, which is never a good sign. He said he was on his way, and I braced for the worst. It's what I do. I'm never optimistic when it comes to these situations. I've had too much experience at trying to persuade myself into thinking nothing's wrong.

A half-hour later, Babba arrived with a stern look on his face, as if someone shot his dog. We came face to face in my kitchen, separated only by a sub wall. He proceeded to tell me Timmy was in trouble. He was referring to Donaghy. I thought to myself what the fuck is he talking about? I just spoke to Tim the day before, and he didn't mention any trouble. The only thing remotely close is that his wife Kim got liposuction two weeks earlier without his knowledge and charged it on the credit card. Other than that, I knew Tim was doing well.

Babba continued to tell me that Donaghy was in real trouble, and word on the street was he could lose his job. I thought, "Holy shit, what did he do this time?" He told me that next time Tim was in Philadelphia for a Sixers game, we needed to meet. I called Tim and set a meeting but never mentioned Battista. He was going to be in Philly the following week, and we agreed to meet at the Airport Marriott in Philadelphia in mid-December 2006.

Soon after that, Battista revealed to me that Donaghy was betting games with which he officiated through a local Delco insurance salesman/ gambler, Jack Concannon, who in turn relayed them to a professional gambler, Pete Ruggieri. I panicked, and my spider senses took over. Was Battista really looking out for Tim's best interest or was there a hidden agenda? The latter made more sense, and I was about to find out. If Donaghy wasn't in trouble at that point, he was about to be.

We pulled up to the entrance of the Marriott, gave the valet twenty bucks and I self-parked my Toyota Corolla right out front; I told him that we were only going to be about an hour. He tucked the twenty in his pocket, and we made our way into the lobby face to face with Donaghy. Timmy was shocked to see Babba. Every ounce of color drained out of his face. Timmy turned to me with a crooked mouth and said, "Tom, what the fuck?" We sat at a table just outside the dining room-Battista and I on one side and Donaghy across from us.

Battista ordered a ton of appetizers. I ordered a shrimp cocktail-under-cooked shrimp cocktail to be precise. We ordered some wine, and it was at that time I realized the magnitude of the moment. We weren't just there to tip Timmy off to the rumors. Babba held up a small, square drink napkin with $2k written on it for two thousand dollars. He proceeded to tell Donaghy that Jack Concannon was making a mint on Tim's games. The two thousand was for every win Donaghy gave us, and he didn't have to pay a dime for a loser. That was a hell of a deal for Babba considering Tim's eventual record of forty wins and five losses. Not to mention the amount of money wagered on his games. Cha-ching! Donaghy was good with it too because according to Tim, Jack was giving Donaghy a mere pittance in comparison to what Jack was raking in.

Donaghy motioned me to the bathroom before he accepted the offer. In the bathroom, Tim splashed water on his face and wiped it dry. I thought he was going to tell me no fucking way, but he told me the complete opposite. He was pissed at Jack for making so much and not giving him his fair share. His exact words were, "Do you believe that mother fucker?" I thought he meant Battista, so I responded, "Who, Babba?" to which he replied, "No, Jack!" I asked him point- blank, "Are you going to do it?" Without missing a beat, Tim said, "Fuck yea!" I was a bit shocked, but, per usual, I went along with everything. I've since stopped that behavior since getting out of the slammer.

For those of you wondering, I'm done being a patsy or pussy if you will. With a son and a beautiful family, I can't afford any more stupid mistakes. We went back to the bargaining table, and Tim, with his lips sealed, nodded his head in agreement. All three of us then left the Marriott, drove to an Essington convenience store, got gas, bought rolling papers and smoked a doobie. It was middies back then, but the best middies money could buy. We got high, drove Timmy back to the Marriott and went home.

Before we dropped Timmy off though, Babba had one small condition. No more Concannon and Ruggieri. Donaghy again nodded in agreement, turned and spoke those infamous words that would begin the greatest scandal in sports history, "Bet Boston tomorrow night against the Sixers." Babba pleaded with us to keep our mouths shut. We agreed and decided on the code word "cranberries" when things went awry.

The Celtics covered, and Tim was 1 and 0 right out of the gate. It was then Battista coined the nickname Elvis for Donaghy. The King! After the game, Tim called me and said, "Good boy," and I responded, "Good boy," and we hung up the phone. It was a ritual we would do following every win. Which, by the way, happened plenty.

The next night, Tim came over my house. Babba walked in with five- thousand dollars, flipped it to Elvis, and said, "Congratulations on your first win!" You might be asking why five thousand when the agreement was two. I suspect it was because Babba was so happy with the first win and must have made a shitload.

I didn't ask questions. I kept my head down and eyes closed until the ride stopped. Before Babba left, Elvis asked, "What about Tommy? Doesn't Tommy get anything?" Babba said, "Don't worry about Tommy, I will take care of him."

Babba always took care of me before the scandal, just not during. He was too busy trying to keep up with what he owed Elvis. His drug habit was also getting out of control. He even fell behind twenty thousand early in the scheme and asked me to front him the money, which I did. It was my pocket that was now light twenty large. Battista left my house, and Tim gave me a thousand of the five thousand dollars that Battista gave him. Timmy always wanted to make sure I was getting something. But Battista's gambling got so bad that he asked me to pay Donagy twenty-thousand out of my own pocket that Donagy was owed. It was another red flag. But I didn't think it would be a problem; I always thought that it would go away the more Timmy won.

Au contraire, the more he won, the more Battista bet (although we didn't know that at the time), and the more pressure there seemed to be for us to win. It became a vicious cycle. I mean, after one game we should have all been rich. You don't win that many games, wager that kind of money, and not walk away a millionaire. Battista kept bitching about Tim's losses, which were few and far between. Another red flag.

I was getting nervous. There was no time to sit and ponder. I had a flight to catch to Phoenix. Tim was refereeing a Suns game, and I had to get his schedule for the month. I strapped twenty- thousand dollars to my ankles and around my waist and boarded a flight for the land of the rising sun. The NBA gave Tim his schedule once a month, which he kept in a binder. I would take a picture of it with my cell phone to have a copy. We did this so when we talked over the phone, there was never any mention of which team to bet.

We then used code words for the home and away teams. Since my brother, Johnny, got married like a damn fool and moved to New Jersey, he was the away team. My other brother, Chuck, stayed in Delco, so he was the home team. Whenever Tim would call on gameday and start talking about one of my brothers, I knew which team we were to bet. I would then call Battista, and he would give me the point spread of the game. I'd call Tim back and mention the point spread in code. A street address or time of the day would suffice. Tim had all he needed. It was now in his hands or, at least, his whistle.

Whenever I ran out of Tim's scheduled games, I flew or drove to where he was, cash in tow. I flew to Toronto with ten- thousand, drove to the Meadowlands with forty-five thousand, took the train to DC with forty more. All on my dime! The trip to the Meadowlands was where I had to come up with twenty- thousand of my own.

We called the money "apples" over the phone. Tim wouldn't continue without his apples, and I didn't blame him one bit. I remember meeting him in the Meadowlands for lunch with two other referees who were oblivious to what was going on. I had the money in a man bag strapped around my waist. After lunch, we went to his room where I dumped the forty-five-thousand on the bed. Tim asked me what I got and I told him the truth, nothing. If he only knew twenty- thousand of it was mine. Tim threw me five-thousand dollars. I wanted to beat the traffic, so I headed home. I had done my job and the scheme continued.

I can give you a roundabout figure of the money we gave Tim during those three-months. There are varying stories on the amount. One was very high and the other very low. I was delivering the stacks, so my mental calculator is much more accurate. It was somewhere in the neighborhood of $100,000. I could be off ten thousand here or there but no more. Being in the middle of things had its advantages and disadvantages. An advantage in that I knew the amount. A disadvantage in that I knew the amount. You figure it out!

The picture on the next page was given to me by Tim Donaghy and signed by Grant Hill. Tim was a great referee, one of the best. I know this because I used to play in a popular pick-up league full of men who could have and should have played at a much higher level but because of certain circumstances, they didn't. I would get so frustrated at the referees. I would often get thrown out for telling a referee he ate shit! They were terrible, and I was competitive. Not a good combo.

One night, Tim called me and asked if I was playing in this league. I answered in the affirmative. They were scrambling for striped shirts, and he wanted to stay sharp. He accepted partly because I'd be on the court. I must tell you; it was then that I got a true appreciation for the talent Tim possessed as a referee. It was the smoothest game I had ever been a part of. He truly was adept at what he did. He was born to referee. Incidentally, this occurred early in Tim's quest to become an NBA referee.

One of many funny stories about Phoenix I have to tell you... Tim and I checked into the Marriott together. Whenever I met him in a city, I stayed in his room. We approached the woman behind the check-in desk, and Tim whispered for me to be quiet. He said, "Hello, I'm from the NHL, and I'm staying two days." Now that I look back on it, we must have looked like two queens at the time. No wonder the prosecuting attorney asked both of us if we were gay. The woman said, "One King or two double beds?" We laughed, and Tim said, "Two doubles, please. He's cute but not that cute." The woman checked us in with the NHL rate, which was about fifteen dollars less than the NBA, which is why Tim told me to be quiet. He did this to cut down on his expenses. He would then submit NBA rates to the NBA for reimbursement.

Before we went to settle in the room and get changed, Tim would bring me to a room in the Marriott where only distinguished guests like Tim were welcome. It was like a VIP room. He said all the referees have access to this room.

He took about ten cans of soda and anything else we could get our hands on back to the room for a feast. Once we got to the room on the twenty-third floor, Tim, always the prankster, went to retrieve the ice bucket. I remember thinking," What the hell is he doing now? He filled the bucket with ice and led me to the balcony. Once on the balcony, Donaghy pointed to the guests dining in the rose garden below. We were so high up they looked like ants.

There it was, plain as day, Donaghy with nothing on but his fruit of the loom tighty whities, a large bucket of ice in his hand, laughing his ass off because he knew what he was about to do. I shouted, "Tim, don't do it, please!" which made him laugh even harder. He then launched the ice over the railing. I remember how long it felt as the ice stayed suspended in the air before falling out of view.

We both leaned over to watch the bombardment, and then it happened. The ice hit the unsuspecting guests like a hail storm. They ran for cover. I turned around, and Tim was gone. I darted back to the room, and there he was curled up in a fetal position in the corner of the room; all I could see was underwear and hairy legs. His mouth ajar; wide open but no sound was coming out because he was laughing so hard. The only time he made a sound was when he inhaled like a barking seal to catch his breath. I had to laugh, even though I had pleaded with him not to do it. He pulled this shit all the time when we were kids, and it didn't stop-even into adulthood.

"They laugh at me because I'm different,
I laugh at them because they're all the same."
Lady Gaga

CHAPTER 6

Pissing Up a Rope

We were about to get pinched.

I could see Babba falling apart right before my eyes. We used to take trips to Atlantic City. Tuesday nights were set aside to play black-jack. We'd often kill two birds with one stone; we played some cards, then paid a visit to a few wise guys to deliver or collect large sums of money. I would chauffeur so he could conduct his business with his laptop and all five phones. Occasionally, I'd have to stop on I-95 in Jersey so Babba could relieve himself.

The Tropicana was our destination. It was Babba's favorite casino, where he was well known as a gambler and treated like a whale (which in the casino world means getting preferential treatment); he was lavished with comps by the house.

While Battista focused on playing blackjack, I walked around the casino, looking to kill time. He often played for hours-that situation left me with a good deal of downtime. I was desperate to find dis-tractions to avoid interrupting Babba's concentration. I did my best to avoid being labeled a jinx or, as the wise guys say, "a mush". The word "mush" was popularized by Robert De Niro in the movie, "A Bronx Tale". This title is not a compliment in gambling and sports communities.

Unfortunately, gamblers who lose or are losing, frequently blame those nearby for their bad luck. To put it in basic terms, being a mush is to create bad luck for others in gambling situations. Losing money sucks big time, so why not blame it on somebody else? After all, it's never the gambler's fault.

On that particular Tuesday night, Babba started losing early.

I came by the poker table a little later to check on him. His glare made it obvious that he was not in the mood for pleasantries. It was equally obvious that my company was not welcome at that point. I took the not-so-subtle hint and left.

Tuesday nights were always quiet in the Tropicana, especially after midnight. I would often head to the Quarter (shown in the picture on the next page) and grab an ice-cream cone; I would sit on a bench and ponder life, asking myself the relevant question, what the hell am I doing here? I had to work the next day, so I always wanted to get home to get enough sleep for the next business day.

On these nights in the Quarter, I would regularly see this beautiful woman, who I thought was a waitress or hostess for the casino. She definitely was not a prostitute, because she didn't charge me a dime that night. We avoided small talk and concentrated on our mutually-shared attraction, We talked for a bit and got down to business. What intensified our encounters was an added element of danger that we might be discovered. We repeated this pattern every Tuesday after that until the Feds showed up on my front doorstep.

I don't know if this encounter was by chance, good luck or Karma but it kept my attention while there was nothing else to do. Sadly, I had to return to the table to find out how much financial trouble

Battista had gotten himself into. I believe that particular night he lost seven- thousand dollars, which made for a long, quiet ride home. Jimmy always shared his winnings, and when he lost, I lost, but on this night, I felt as though I had won, after all, I had just gotten laid!

Babba was also spending more time at my house lately; sleeping over every night and growing a bit paranoid. I enjoyed his company, plus I could see something was wrong. His wife was blowing up my phone constantly, and he told me, "Whatever you do, don't answer the phone." He gave me his reasons not to answer, but they didn't make sense. One day, while working at JPMorgan, she got a hold of me through my personal assistant. I picked up the phone and a crackling voice said, "Tommy, Jimmy is in trouble. He owes many millions of dollars to people who you don't want to owe." She mentioned that he was playing online poker and/or blackjack until the wee hours of the morning and lost a shitload of money. That explained everything, well not everything, but it explained why I had to cough up twenty grand and why he had no money to pay Elvis.

I went home that evening and told him I had talked to Debbie. He said, "What the fuck did she say?" I told him exactly. The following day, her family showed up at my house and took him off to rehab. He told me Pete Ruggieri would be in touch and take over while he was away. That was when Pete showed up at JPMorgan with his two beautiful children and mentioned the lost chance with the guaranteed lottery winner. From here on out, I was dealing with Pete until our inevitable bust.

I met Pete at the local CVS. I told him right off the bat how Tim was owed mucho apples and wouldn't continue without it. Pete said," I'll be over your house this week with money for Tim." He was owed around forty-five-thousand at the time. Incidentally, at one point in the scheme , Tim's amount per game went from two-thousand to five-thousand because he was doing so well. Pete was amazed at how little Donaghy was getting and increased it to ten-thousand. He was also astonished that I was paying for my travel whenever I met Donaghy. The pittance I did get was from Tim's cut.

Pete insisted that the stinginess would cease and that the upcoming year would be a banner one for the new trio. No Battista. I suspect Pete knew there was no next year, but said it anyway. I guess to throw me off. At this point, I believe, Pete was on the very inside of the game!

Pete arrived at my house one warm afternoon wearing a sweat suit. I thought it was strange, but maybe it was customary for Pete to dress so warmly on a hot day. He dropped thirty-thousand on my kitchen table. All $100 bills. I said, "Pete, that's not going to do it. Tim won't give us another game unless he has all the money owed to him." I also let Pete know that I had to put up twenty grand myself to give to Donaghy. He assured me he'd be back the next day with the rest.

He asked me a million questions that afternoon that were even more suspicious than the warm-up suit and he was acting scared - nervous as hell, which, in turn, made me nervous. He was sweating and stuttering a little, almost as if he were wearing a wire. I believe he was but can't prove it. I had the feeling Pete had flipped. After he left, I called Battista in rehab, and he assured me Pete was on the up and up. I was right, Babba was wrong.

My spider senses were correct yet again. Pete returned the next evening with the rest of the money plus my twenty-thousand out of pocket and another ten for the effort. I don't blame Peter for what he had to do. I would have done it a million times over. He had the most to lose, and I could see why he would be pissed at how everything went down.

I never knew the details of exactly how we got caught, but a recent article in ESPN Magazine March 2019 edition has a timeline of events leading up to the meeting at the Marriott. To my surprise, the author of the article states that Battista met with a South Florida bookmaker named Taylor "Popeye" Breton at a Phillies-Yankees game at Citizens Bank Park in June 2006. That's around five to six months before my role in the scandal ever started. At that meeting, Babba revealed to Popeye that he had a ref on his payroll and carelessly stated his name as Tim Donaghy. We were done, and we hadn't even started; we were pissing up a rope. and trouble was on the horizon.

Knowing the truth was important to me and my family. The past twelve years have been riddled with questions about our ultimate "pinch". That was closure for me; the pieces of the puzzle were finally in place. Some questions still exist, but that was the one that helped me finally rest my head on the pillow.

"I'm a kind person, I'm kind to everyone, but if you are unkind to me, then kindness is not what you'll remember me for."
Al Capone

CHAPTER 7

The Perjury Trap

One week later, while I was sitting on the sand in South Beach Miami, an unavailable number appeared on my phone. With all the shit going on, I was praying it was a telemarketer, but every criminal knows an unavailable number is either the Feds or a wrong number. It was the FBI, Paul Harris and Jerry Conrad, to be exact, and they said that they were standing on my front porch. Why would they be there when they knew where I was? They were trying to ruin my vacation. It's what they do best, ruin shit. Mission accomplished, pricks!

That beautiful dinner I had planned that night was no more. My appetite was gone. I was a mess but still hoping they had questions about Battista's criminal activity and not Donaghy. My spider senses took over again. Back in action and batting a thousand. It had to be about Donaghy; all the signs were there.

Pete Ruggieri sweating and nervously asking questions, referring to the winning lottery -ticket and the whispers of a wiretap. Now the FBI's was on my front porch. I told them, "I'll be home next week." They said, "We'll see you on Thursday." Then came the knock at the door: pain in the ass, Paul Harris and nice guy, Jerry Conrad. Just like in the movies. Good cop, bad cop. Only thing was that Paul couldn't act a lick. I could teach him a thing or two about acting or get him in touch with my good buddy Scott Wolf.

Now I know it's the FBI's job to be annoying, but this guy takes the cake. Showing up at my brother's business who incidentally had nothing to do with the scandal, pulling out handcuffs and said in front of all the gawking bystanders to hear, "Next time you see Tommy, tell him I'm going to put these on him." Paul was trying to ruin my brother's business? And he was an innocent guy! Paul Harris went around my neighborhood, knocking on doors asking people about me so that I would find out. He showed them pictures of my niece and me that he found on Facebook. One of my neighbors thought I was a child molester as a result. My one neighbor, Ray, told him, "Tommy's a good guy." Paul's response was, "Good guys end up in jail." Well Paul, so do FBI agents. So, reread your manual and brush up on your skills. You missed your calling, buddy. I think you'd be better off in a local mall or a carnival to be quite honest with you. Sorry if I got off the subject but, according to Donaghy, Phil Scala was quoted as saying, "Martino was the weirdest little guy I ever met." Well Phil, have you ever met Paul Harris? They showed up on my front porch, and like a dumb ass, I invited them in. Never invite FBI agents in your home. They started rifling off questions like a howitzer. Not coincidentally, they were the same questions Pete Ruggieri had asked me two weeks earlier. That's when I was 99.9 percent sure Pete was on the take.

The Philadelphia Phillies could surely use me in their leadoff spot with my batting average but, instead, I was headed to NYC to testify, and they were months away from the World Series. I walked them out to the front porch, and Harris handed me the subpoena to appear before a grand jury. I asked nicely if I could plead the fifth right now, or is that something I gotta show up in person to do? They said, "We'll see you in Brooklyn in two weeks." I was then made aware that whoever cooperates and provides information first gets the best deal. When they walked across my lawn, I gave them the Italian gesture of the middle finger with my right hand slapping the inside of my left bicep and forearm and said under my breath "Vaffanculo!" I did that when they weren't looking, of course. This is the Italian way we say "Fuck off!"

To make matters worse, the Feds had another weapon in their arsenal. They had an FBI agent in their hip pocket who lived at the entrance of my cul-de-sac. He once gave me a royal blue t-shirt with FBI across the chest in white capital letters. I later used it as a cum rag after they pissed me the hell off. His name was AJ, and he was funneling information back to New York. I also learned that he was taking down license-plate numbers of anyone near or affiliated with my home. They even knew my friend Jimmy Barbacane took me to the airport one morning as I headed off to the Bahamas. I'm sure AJ played a role in that revelation.

They never asked a question to which they didn't know the answer. They made a point of asking my friend, Spike, during his questioning, "Who took Tommy to the airport?" Irrelevant to the case but a way of testing his authenticity. I thought AJ was my friend, but no FBI agent is ever your friend, trust me. They will make it appear as if they are only to extract information. They use it to move up in the organization and pat themselves on the back.

Battista made yet another blunder as he had a habit of doing. Babba haphazardly struck up a conversation with AJ where Babba described what he was doing at my house every day. He said, "I'm Tommy's friend and a professional gambler. Tommy lets me work from his house in peace and quiet." He then asked AJ where he was from. AJ told him the Carolinas. Battista shot back, "I'll work on Carolina Panthers-Eagles tickets for you in the front row at the fifty-yard line." AJ was pleased about the tickets, according to Battista. The next time I saw AJ, he asked multiple questions about Babba. He later told me that he had to call headquarters in compliance with his job and inform them of what he found out about Babba. AJ treated me like a criminal from that point on.

It was close to Halloween around the time of my self-surrender. AJ was playing with his kids in the cul-de-sac. I pulled up and rolled the window down because I had bought his children Halloween bags for their candy collection. He took a step away from my car, held his hands up and said rudely, "I'm not accepting that". I drove to my home with such a sick feeling in my stomach. What a complete dick. Take them and throw them out but don't act like I have leprosy. They were beautiful Halloween-candy bags with a big jack-o-lantern adorning each side. I purchased several at the dollar store for the kids in the neighborhood.

Incidentally, when I got home from the halfway house, AJ no longer was a resident of our cul-de-sac. I saw him at a local Wawa convenience store up the street from my house recently. He moved away while I was in jail. He had done his job, so he rolled. To my surprise, he apologized, and I accepted. He told me he got sick with some type of cancer. I hope he's doing well. Whether it was small or large, he had a hand in assisting his comrades, otherwise, an apology wouldn't be in order. I haven't seen him since.

Back to Harris and Conway, I had to get an attorney fast. It cost me five-thousand dollars as a retainer to travel to Brooklyn to testify. It sounds as ominous as it was. I was frightened beyond belief. Before heading into the jury room, my attorney advised me to plead the fifth on everything except the easy questions like where you live and your name and address. Not coincidentally, my lawyer was appointed to me by Battista's attorney, Jack McMahon.

When I walked into the room, there was a Judge, twelve jurors, a stenographer and the prosecuting attorney, Tom Segal, from the eastern district of New York. He had a stack of papers and an angry look on his face. He was an intimidating dude who was out to get me. He peppered me with questions, one after another, starting with the name and address. The questions didn't stop. I answered one after another after another. When I was answering a question, he was asking two more and taking my answers for whatever question he wanted.

Without provocation, he stopped the proceedings and shouted, "You all heard that! He just lied." The Judge nodded her head in agreement. He asked the stenographer if she recorded that, and she nodded also. He then turned to the jury, "Did you all hear that?" They all nodded yes out of fear. I thought the whole mess was rigged. What did I lie about? He had my phone records in his hand and asked me what Tim and I were talking about for so long on the phone each night. I said, "Family matters. My brother knows his brother, I know his wife, he knows my brothers, etc."

Since I knew his real motivation for asking, I obstructed the process and deliberately made things difficult for him. It wasn't a lie. I did talk to Tim about family matters. How was that a lie? More like a perjury trap. A Rigged Game. I had no idea because I'd never been in trouble before, and I was misinformed. If they say I committed perjury, then I committed perjury. There was no turning back. They were all in on it together. I didn't stand a chance that day unless I plead the fifth on everything, including my name and address. I was fucked, and as I was led out, Tom Segal approached me and said, "Your friend Tim refereed his last NBA game. Count on it!"

The Feds then went after my family to get to me. They subpoenaed my brother, Chuck, to the grand jury and audited his hair salon. They accused me of laundering money through his business. They knew we weren't but were trying to squeeze me by harassing family members. I advised Chuck on the correct way to plead the fifth. The hair salon's audit was carried out and confirmed. We met and exceeded all the quality system-management requirements but it ended up costing my brother $17,000 for the trip to New York. They were going for our pocketbooks too, trying to bleed us dry, and they were succeeding.

Mom was next. Do you think they considered her health problems? Not giving a shit was an art form to these jokers! My girlfriend pleaded the fifth. When she left the courtroom, she was told she'd never see her daughter again. Another scare tactic that sent her back in to accept a proffer. Another $7,000 later and they had exactly what they wanted. Her guts were all over that floor, spilled like a toddler's glass of milk at dinner-any chance I had of getting leniency went out the door. I couldn't be with her after that, so I lost her number.

The legal definition of a proffer is a written agreement between federal prosecutors and individuals under criminal investigation, which allows these individuals to give the government information about crimes with some assurances of protection against prosecution. My mother testifying was out of the question, and I needed the perjury charged reduced somehow. It was survival time, and I switched to survival mode. They were attacking my family and our finances and NOBODY, especially my co-defendant, offered me a dime to help cover his ass like I was doing. No more protecting people who don't share my last name!

I notified my attorney, Vicki Herr. It was time to agree to a proffer and head to Brooklyn. Incidentally, Vicki Herr did a remarkable job representing me, and I won't ever forget it. She put her heart and soul into the case, and it showed at sentencing. If it weren't for her, I would have been looking at more time. The late Fred Shero once said to his players after they won the Stanley Cup, "We will walk together forever". And Vicki and I will! So, off to Brooklyn we went for five consecutive days. We drove some and took the metro liner others. It was torture and expensive, and the Feds were intentionally leaking confidential information to the news media so it would get back to us. The hope was that we'd hit the panic button and rush in to get a deal. I remember on the way home from Brooklyn one day on the train, after facing questioning from Tom Segal and many FBI agents for hours, Vicki Herr got a call from the New York Post informing her that someone got caught on a wiretap saying they had an NBA ref in their hip pocket while the Feds were investigating the Gambino crime family. That could have only come from one source, the FBI. Like I said earlier, if they want you, they get you.

Those sessions in New York were draining. They had boxes all over the room, filled with paper. Mob names written on them as a scare tactic and a tape recorder in the center of the table. They asked me thousands of questions, mostly about Donaghy. He was telling them one thing, and I was telling them another. I had the truth on my side. The Feds knew but would never admit to it. That would have to result in a lighter sentence for me or a change in stance on Donaghy.

They asked me how much I made a week selling weed. I told them the truth, which was not easy to figure out. I gave them a roundabout figure, but Donaghy was telling them an inflated number. They were calling me a liar. How would Donaghy know my weed-selling income? They should have asked me how much I made on a pound of weed. Now that's a legitimate question, but none of them smoked weed I'm sure. If they did, they would have asked more pertinent questions and would have been much more relaxed. They even asked

Donaghy and me if we were gay. I thought it was irrelevant to the case, so I told them I would be whatever they wanted me to be. Vicki Herr interjected and assured them that I was not gay.

There was one question they wouldn't let rest. It's essential to the story and something that Tim and I still haggle over to this day. They wanted to know the amount of money I had given to Donaghy and, in particular, the payments Ruggieri gave me in my kitchen. Tim told them I had kept it, and I told them the truth: I had given it to Donaghy. They played the game of telling me I had taken it and that I was a bullshitter. I stuck to my word. I even told them I'd take a polygraph. Their response? "Only liars say that." What the fuck kind of game were they playing? I'm sure that was Paul Harris who blurted that one out.

During the questioning, Harris mentioned something about Ruggieri to me. I believe it was, "Tommy, are you afraid of Ruggieri?" Now they had never mentioned Pete at all until this gaffe by Harris. The room went silent. Someone kicked Harris from under the table, and he tried to cover up by saying something stupid like, "I mean, Pete's an intimidating guy." He never opened his mouth again after that. They should have put a muzzle on this guy from the beginning. I knew then what I already realized when I first met the guy. They didn't want Pete's name mentioned ever. It was an eye-opener for me. For some reason, they were protecting Pete. We know the reason, but at the time, I wasn't 100% positive of the exact role Pete played. I didn't give a rat's ass either way. I knew someday I would find out. It's still not totally clear, though.

My father often asks about Ruggieri and Concannon. What happened to them? No charges? Immunity? More importantly, to the Feds, though, was the money Ruggieri gave to me in my kitchen. They asked me, "If you gave it to Donaghy, where is it?" I had an answer. Donaghy told me he had it hidden in his attic above the garage, so his wife Kim wouldn't find it. Yahtzee! Tim told them the week before where he hid his money, and the stories matched. They started to realize I was telling the truth.

I never understood why they kept asking where that final payment to Donaghy went. It was clear to me; I gave it to Tim. Maybe they're not omnipotent like they claim. They must have assigned that duty to Harris unless the money or part of the money Pete gave me in my kitchen was federal cash.

Tim told me recently, and several times since getting out of jail, that he wrote them a check for thirty- thousand dollars. Now, why would Donaghy have to write them a check for anything? The answer was simple; they wanted their money back. They wasted enough time and money on this wild goose chase. I gave them clarity and tied up all the loose ends for them.

The second to the last question they asked me went like this, "Okay Martino, this is important, were these really three high-school buddies who got together and bet Donaghy's games?" I said, "Yes, we were. ." That was it. They wrapped things up. Then something odd happened. A handsome gentleman, who didn't say a word through-out the entire interrogation, sat at the end of the table. He stood up, approached me and asked about Danny Malatesta.

Danny is a childhood friend who served time in Fort Dix, New Jersey but was not involved in the scandal. I'm assuming he asked about Danny because to connect the scandal with organized crime. I responded, "Danny is on the up and up from what I understand.". He said, "Okay. Thank you, my friend." He bent over and whispered in my ear, "I believe you!" I remember his face, but they never mentioned his name. It was Phil Scala, head of the task force in charge of the investigation into the Gambino crime family. It was the first thing anyone said to me in weeks that was positive, and I appreciated it. Off to sentencing.

"People, even more than things, have to be restored, renewed, revived, reclaimed and redeemed... Never throw out anybody."
Audrey Hepburn

CHAPTER 8

Judgment Day

Sentencing was something that no one ever wants to face. Vicki Herr braced me for the worst. She said, "Tommy, you're going to jail." Words I hated to hear, but she was telling it like it was. I believe my guidelines were between six to sixteen months. Not bad, but one hour in the clink sucks, let alone months. The judge can deliver whatever sentence she wants. We were all praying for probation, but that wasn't going to happen. The NBA was involved, and the judge had to send a clear message. Don't fuck with the NBA.

So many people sent beautiful letters to the judge, pleading for leniency. I was getting what I was getting, no matter how many wrote letters for me. They should have been written on toilet paper so they could wipe their ass with them. What a waste of paper. Those poor trees.

My family went with me that fateful day. It was the first time I saw my brother, Johnny, cry. His little brother was going away for a while. If the roles had been reversed, I would've felt the same way. There's no way to explain what went through my head that day. I had enough of that ride to Brooklyn and the city of Brooklyn itself. It was time to get this over with once and for all. The system was rigged anyway. The judges know the prosecutors who know the stenographers who know the bailiffs, etc. Jesus, they're all from New York and work in the same building every day. They all know one another. The deck was stacked in their favor. Talk about the Mob.

The judicial system was as corrupt as we were. At one point, the prosecuting attorney didn't know what to charges to bring against me. They needed additional time to figure it out-a charge that would stick. The judge gave them as much time as they needed. I believe it was a couple of days. You would think the judge would be suspicious of this, but it was standard practice. They pulled a rabbit out of their ass and charged me with wire fraud- using my cell phone to cheat the NBA out of the honest services of a referee.

Don't forget, I still had the perjury charge hanging out of my ass sideways. Every other week on the news, I see an innocent person released from jail after spending twenty to thirty years of incarceration. I attribute it to our corrupt, and backward, judicial system.

I used to wonder when I saw the accused on TV if they were really guilty. Then I went through the "process." Now I know, there are many innocent people in jail – some whose crimes don't match the sentence. Hard-working taxpayers who go away because of a corrupt judge or the prosecuting attorney or both. It sucks, but our hands are tied. I'm not saying that our judge was corrupt, but she sure as hell lacked empathy-something absent in most judges anyway. I could've given her CPR following a heart attack and she still would have assigned me an orange jumpsuit. Any hope my family had of me getting probation was out the window once they assigned this judge to our case. My attorney was right, "You're going to jail, Tommy. It's just a matter of how long."

I remember sitting in a squad car outside the building where the sentencing was to take place, and the nice officer put the radio on, so I could hear what was going on. It was a local news station covering the sentencing. Battista and I were sentenced together because we were co-defendants. Our relationship, however, got tattered in the months leading up to sentencing. They were offering us plea deals. Battista wanted to go to trial. We all knew he was bluffing, especially the prosecution. He wanted a lighter sentence and believed they had no case against him.

They had me for perjury, so I was fucked. They tacked on wire fraud for good measure. They were prepared to drop my perjury charge for obstruction had Babba agreed to an allegation of gambling charge. Initially, Battista rebuked the offer, which sent my family into a rage. He later accepted the gambling charge. I remember the radio personality saying, "Okay, it's time for Battista and Martino to get sentenced." He put the car in drive and headed to the back of the building where paparazzi flooded the streets. They snuck us in with police escorts as we headed to the courtroom; it was packed to the gills. If I were going to get the book thrown at me at least I wanted to look good so I wore my five- thousand-dollar Trussini suit.

I saw people I knew from ESPN and the New York Post and, of course, my family. That worst part was the fact that my family had to endure the torture of seeing their favorite son sentenced to jail. I now understood what it was like to have an out of body experience. I let everyone down-even my dog, Macie. From my dog to my good-for-nothing shit-bird, temporary girlfriend I had at the time. No wonder I used so many escort services. The best part about escorts is they bring condoms with them and leave after an hour. Then again, if it weren't for that shit-bird girlfriend, I would have never met my beautiful bride.

We sat down in the courtroom as quiet as church mice in a library. I sat next to Battista, as illustrated in the courtroom sketch on the next page. Our lawyers made us read an apology in the hope the judge would sympathize with us. She put the screws to us anyway. It's a weird, archaic system and procedure. We were going through the motions. I read my apology, choked up as I glanced at my dad in the back of the courtroom. Battista followed with his. Both were rehearsed and phony. We sat back down; the judge scolded us, and our sentences were handed down. Battista got fifteen months, and I got a year and a day. They tacked on restitution to the NBA for $217,000, based on Donaghy's NBA salary. Initially, the number was way above the million-dollar mark; however, Vicki Herr came to our rescue.

The restitution to the NBA should be in the amount of Donaghy's salary but not his entire salary because the scandal only lasted three months. So, the restitution should be prorated over the course of those three months. The judge agreed. If I could put an emoji in this book of clapping hands, I would because Vicki Herr deserves a round of applause for that one or a standing ovation. If not for her, we would be fucked right now.

I want to say something about my sentence. What's that extra day about? Here's why: a federal-prison inmate can only receive "good-time" credit (early release) of up to fifty-four days for displaying "exemplary compliance with institutional disciplinary regulations" if his or her sentence is more than a year. So, the sentence of a year and a day is a judicial gift. I didn't classify it this way because, under federal law, and in most states, a misdemeanor is a criminal offense that carries a possible jail term of less than one year. I would have rather gotten 364 days and not had the felony on my record. It's a catch 22.

Additionally, when inmates find out you're doing a year and a day, it puts you in jeopardy. Immediately, the sentence signals cooperation. The month of good time wasn't worth the torture I endured in jail with inmates calling me a snitch. That being said, I was off to jail but not right away. The judge gave us time to get our affairs in order. I was sentenced in July 2008 and had to self-surrender October 15th of the same year.

Vicki Herr informed the judge that I'd be graduating from cosmetology school in September and that I was "on the path to redemption". The judge reminded Vikki and me that my path would run through a Federal prison. That prison would turn out to be MDC Brooklyn. Tempers flared after the hearing when my brother Johnny confronted Battista. Johnny blamed Battista for "exploiting" my "good nature" and having me serve as a bagman for the operation. "Do your own God damn dirty work," he screamed at a visibly frightened Battista. Nevertheless, Babba and I were headed to the same prison in Brooklyn and would be on the same floor but in different units, 54 and 53, respectively.

In the months before self-surrendering, Vicki put in a request to the judge for the two of us to be assigned different prisons. We should have gotten a response within seven days of the application but heard nothing. Later in my incarceration, I received a letter granting me the right to a different camp other than MDC Brooklyn. This is a prime example of how fucked up the system was and still is. They wanted me in Brooklyn come hell or high water.

> *"You can do a million good things, and no one remembers. If you do one bad thing no one forgets."*
> Thomas Martino

CHAPTER 9

MDC BROOKLYN,
Federal Bureau of Prisons
(A rat-infested dump)

It was kind of the judge to let us get our affairs in order. Being sent off to prison right away is cruel. I appreciated that because I had so many loose ends to attend to. I had to drop off my dog to my mom's. I did it the night before I had to surrender. When I dropped Macie off, she was a skinny little pug. When I got her back a year later, she was a fat, little piggy. I wish I could say the same for yours truly. My mom stuffed her like a turkey while I was gone.

I also had to make plans with my house and my bills. My dad took care of all my financial matters. Dad paid my bills while I was gone and put enough away to jump-start my life again upon release. My father told me about the sum of money during a visit. I had been in the "Hole" or SHU (Special Housing Unit) in Brooklyn. Like I said before, if it weren't for dad, well, I don't even want to think about that scenario. I had to winterize my house and have someone check it periodically.

I had a girlfriend at the time who had many boyfriends that I didn't know about. She was supposed to hold down the fort while I was away, but that lasted about a week. What little money I had left, I entrusted to my longtime friend and confidant, Jim Kennedy who I affectionately referred to as the "K-Man". I had around forty-five-thousand dollars left to my name.

All of my legal fees and expenses totaled close to half-a-million. Cosmetology school alone was fifteen thousand. I had a big-shot lawyer in New York City for one week who charged me ten-thousand dollars. His assistant would call me and I'd get a bill for two hundred and fifty dollars. Whenever my phone would ring and it was a New York number I'd cringe because I knew a large bill would follow the phone call.

K-Man agreed to meet me at the Towne House Restaurant in Media Pennsylvania. I was scared shitless. If you are ever followed for a period of time, the rest of your life you'll be looking over your shoulder. That's precisely what I was doing. I was paranoid off the Richter Scale. In the back of the restaurant on the side of the bar area was a phone booth where I summoned K-Man. We entered and closed the door behind us. I pulled a knot of hundreds wrapped in rubber bands from my waistband. K-man couldn't believe his eyes as he exclaimed, "Wooooow". That was a load off my back. Jimmy could be trusted.

When I did finally get home from the joint, he had every dime waiting for me. One of the worst things about going away to prison is the self-surrender. My buddy, Spike, and my brother, Johnny, drove me to Brooklyn in the morning hours of October 15th 2008-the day of reckoning. I remember I had a cuckoo clock in my kitchen that would make the cuckoo noise every hour. On a regular night, I might hear it once at midnight. On this night in October, I heard it every hour on the hour. I didn't sleep a wink, which wasn't a good thing.

The sun came up, and I was wide awake – weary but awake. My entourage showed up early and whisked me out of Delco. We headed up I-95 to Brooklyn. My cell phone blew up with words of encouragement from friends and family during the trek. One meaningful call came from Russell Perry, one of the nicest guys in the world-a true gentleman who is a friend to this day. He attended my wedding in Key West Florida, my second home. I shed many a tear on that lonely ride to Brooklyn, but Russell, in particular, softened the blow.

When we finally reached the prison, we noticed we were about an hour early. I wasn't stupid enough to spend an extra minute in that place if I didn't have to, so we decided to get a slice of pizza across the street. I don't know if you've ever had a slice of pizza in Brooklyn or maybe we just got lucky, but this was ridiculous. It was thin and crispy, just how I like it. You could hold the pizza in the air, and it wouldn't move a millimeter. Even this pizza couldn't get my mind off of what was awaiting me across the street behind the trestle.

It was an ominous-looking building, and I could hear inmates yelling at the top of their lungs from the windows above. I remember there was a booth with a person inside. It resembled an old phone booth, only bigger. It reminded me of the ticket booth at a carnival where you pay to get on the rides. Next to that hut was a sliding gate adorned with barbed wire (pictured on the next page). It wasn't what everybody described to me as a camp. This wasn't a minimum-security prison with dormitory living. Where was the Club FED they promised me? It was a maximum-security prison disguised as a camp. I was in for one hell of a year.

The woman in the booth opened the barbed-wire gates and pointed to a grey door on a huge brick building as she commanded, "Go knock on that door." I shit my pants for a second time, then knocked on the door. Two black women came out, and I asked "Where is the camp?" They laughed and said, "You're standing in it." I thought she meant the pile of shit that just dropped out of my sweatpants. Instead, she meant the pile of shit I was about to enter. I knew I was in trouble, but I had to toughen up right then. It was the first day. I hadn't even entered the building yet, but I knew I was fucked.

Supposedly I was in Brooklyn because you do time where you did the crime and because the Gambinos were from Brooklyn. But why didn't Donaghy? They were clearly sending me a message. I was entering the closest thing to hell on earth, and there was no turning back. I was approached by a large, armed man who told me to take off my clothes. I obliged. I had to do the bend over and look up my ass deal you hear about in the movies.

He brought over a large hamper with wheels and told me to pick out something that fit.

Well, I got news for you, nothing fit. The underwear was oversized and stood up on their own. Everything smelled like cheap laundry detergent. The shade of orange just wasn't me. I haven't seen XL since learning about Roman numerals in third grade. The jumpsuit was so baggy that I had to roll up the pant legs. They barely reached my crotch area, and I still tripped when I walked. He led me to a holding cell where I sat for what felt like four hours. Without the luxury of clocks, there was no way to determine how long I waited there. In prison, all you have is time, so it becomes an obsession. The bench I sat on was metal and as cold as a popsicle. Inmates were ushered in, single file, some laughing contentedly. They must have been lifers or homeless outside of prison.

Then I was taken to a room to get fingerprinted. They took pictures of us without our clothes on. Finally, a prison guard escorted me to a well-known holding facility in MDC Brooklyn. It is here where they test you for diseases, including AIDS and hepatitis. I was seated amidst murderers and drug cartels. There was caution tape on a cell on the upper floor. I asked an inmate what happened, and he told me there was a rape last evening. White-collar criminals? Work cadre? Club FED? I think not!

My first cellmate or "bunkie" as we like to say was a cartel who didn't speak a lick of English. We would try to communicate for hours to understand each other for one minute. I still don't know what his crime was. The holding facility was for inmates awaiting trial. I was playing chess one day with this bald guy, Spivey, who was beating everyone. It was a competitive game until he asked what I was in for. I told him, and he stood up and shouted "Hey, we got a celebrity here!" It was kind of funny until I asked him why he was here. He told me double murder as I quickly moved my king into checkmate and fled the scene.

Spivey was waiting forever for a catheter after using the same one for a week. That's how bad it was. MDC Brooklyn consistently provided inadequate medical care, not to mention the occasional rat sightings and cockroaches. We very rarely saw the light of day. I remember the rec deck (shown below), which had mesh grates adorned with 10-foot-high walls that allowed inmates some fresh air. At one point, late in the day, you could touch sunlight. Boy, was that a treat. It lasted only for a brief moment, but how else was I supposed to get any vitamin D? The rec deck consisted of half-court basketball with no net, of course, a wall ball court and pull-up bars.

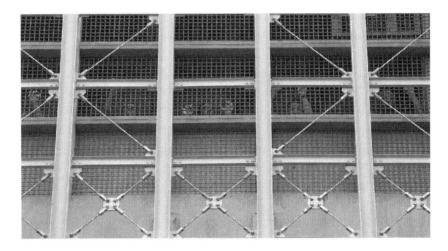

The food at MDC Brooklyn was fake and inedible. I remember the chicken sandwiches were like rubber and if you peeled back the breading, the chicken was grey and resembled a frozen hamburger patty. My buddy, Larry Crites, loved them, so I would trade him my chicken sandwich for his cornbread. The cornbread was edible but definitely way past its expiration date. Stale cornbread was a delicacy at MDC Brooklyn. Larry was doing twenty-four months extorting money from two men in the Taunton, Massachusetts area. The plot was engineered by Anthony St. Laurent, Sr., a member of the Rhode Island Patriarca crime family.

This prison wasn't like any other. It's designed to break you. I never got the proper medication that I needed to survive. I have asthma and needed my albuterol. I never saw it. The CO called my name, and I was off to what I thought was my final resting place. Boy, was I wrong. It was unit fifty-three and, as luck would have it, I was assigned unit manager, Ramsheram. Inmates were praying that they wouldn't get "Ram". When I arrived at unit fifty-three, it felt like I had just walked into a bad neighborhood. I didn't know what to do; they gave me zero direction. No one gave a shit here. It was prison. Why the hell would I expect anyone to? MDC Brooklyn was once perfectly described as a place to warehouse human beings.

Before I could make my way across the unit floor, an enormous Latino inmate approached me and handed me shower shoes. His name was Lantigua, and I thought to myself, "Wow, that was nice." Stay tuned. The shower shoes were enormous but would work better than bare feet until I ordered my own that fit. You needed shower shoes because the cement floors in the shower stalls were disgusting. You can just imagine what goes down those drains. If I didn't have shower shoes on, my feet might get pregnant.

If you saw the movie *Bad Boys* with Sean Penn, that's exactly how the unit looked. Two tiers with lunch benches and several TV's in the common area. When I looked around, I saw a variety of people. They were from all walks of criminal life: drug dealers, a handful of organized-crime fellows and just a few white-collar guys.

The wise guys were in Babba's unit just across the walkway. They were good to me. One of my first assignments was to head to the laundry room for uniforms-whites for work, greens for hanging out and khakis for visitors. An Asian man, who stood with a clipboard with names of inmates arriving on it and who would eventually become my bunkie, summoned two other inmates and me to the laundry room. I gave my name, and he looked up and said, "Martino?" I said, "Yes." He then responded, "We've been waiting for you. Go over to Carmine and pick out your clothes."

There was a sharp-looking, older man standing there with well-groomed hair and a dark complexion. I would later find out he and his son were made men in the Gambino crime family, which means they were stone-cold killers. There were also members of the Lucchese family as well in MDC Brooklyn. Since the Gambinos made plenty of money on Donaghy's bets, I got preferential treatment- thanks to Babba. He told them I was coming and that they should take care of me.

Carmine was an Italian man standing quietly amongst the haberdashery. He motioned me over with a wave and a smile. He looked at all the new clothes and said, "Pick what you want, Martino." The clothes were new and had never been worn. The other two guys got to pick from the shit wagon. They later asked me, "What the fuck just happened?" I even got new shoes. The others were old and wet- soaked actually. When I eventually got to my cell, there was a jar of peanut butter and one of jelly on my bunk, courtesy of Babba.

I also received a brand new pair of sneakers that fit like a glove; they were tucked under my bed. I got to meet my bunkie. He was a big, black guy nicknamed Fammo because he was like family to everyone. He was a cool dude, and I was happy to be his bunkie-right up until it was time to go to bed.

The new guy always sleeps on the top bunk. At around 11 p.m., I laid my head on the pillow for a much-deserved night's sleep. I hadn't slept since the night before the cuckoo clock. That was about ten days ago. Every ten minutes or so, the heat would kick in and blow right on my face. The smell from the vent was one of ammonia-a recipe for disaster for someone afflicted with asthma. Something in that vent was causing my asthma to rear its ugly head, and I had no medication to combat an attack.

A couple of days later, I told Fammo I had to switch to another cell. Turns out Fammo worked as a custodian and every day would spray disinfectant into the vent. It was a concoction he came up with himself. Once he realized it was affecting my breathing, he ceased the spraying. See what I mean by family?

Unfortunately, it was too late for me to stay as his bunkie. When you have asthma that vent may as well have been home to a bevy of animal carcasses. That smell was never going away. Any little thing triggers my asthma. I once went on a horse and buggy ride in New Hope, Pennsylvania with my new, beautiful bride Ashley. Something from the horse's ass was making my face blow up like a balloon. I couldn't breathe. I forced the driver to pull over. I got off, took a Benadryl and plenty of allergy eye drops. It took about two days, but I fully recovered.

Unfortunately, I couldn't breathe in Fammo's bunk and was moved to another cell with the Asian fellow who manned the clipboard in the laundry room. I finally had a name for the face, Steve Yi. If it weren't for that vent, it would have worked with Fammo. One last story before I put Fammo to bed: there was an openly-gay Hispanic guy who went by the name J-Lo. I had to wait a week before I could get transferred to another bunk, They don't do what you want whenever you want in MDC Brooklyn. It's quite the opposite.. I was sitting by myself at lunch this one day, when J-Lo sat down across from me. I didn't know what to think. Maybe he didn't have friends, which would be odd since I knew this wasn't true because everyone liked him. He walked like a girl, talked like a girl, and he even looked like a girl. He might as well have been a girl. He probably was a girl but just didn't have the correct utensils. He was a funny and cool dude. He would perform sexual acts on inmates in our unit; his cell entry was a revolving door at times. Larry and I would watch from a distance. Nothing to see-just traffic in and out.

During our lunch, J-Lo started questioning me about my lifestyle-what I did for a living?. Was I ever married? Was I currently married? Did I have a girlfriend? Etc. We talked for about an hour that day, and I just blew it off thinking it was just another strange event that happens in MDC Brooklyn. We went about our business and were friends from there on out.

Later in my stay, Fammo stops me, pulls me aside and said, "Tommy, I owe you an apology." I looked at him quizzically as he continued, "Do you remember your lunch date with J-Lo? Well, I set that up to make sure you weren't gay, seeing as though you were going to be my bunkie. It's something that I needed to know. It's evident you're not, but I just wanted to apologize." I thought, "Wow! Fammo is the man, and family is definitely his game!" He made sure I knew that J-Lo reported back to him and said, "Honey, I got the best gaydar on the planet and let me tell you that boy is not gay." Fammo and I were tight from there on out.

Pickup basketball games on the rec deck were very competitive. I may be short in stature but, as I've written earlier, the sporting arena is where I stand tall. During one game, MDC player, T-Mac, slammed me into the brick wall driving to the basket, and I cut my chin. Several stitches were required. They called that type of basketball, jail ball. It was hack city, but Larry and I won that contest.

During my visit to the infirmary, I met Peter Gotti the former head of the Gambino crime family and brother of the late John Gotti. He was balding with gray hair, wore round glasses and walked with a cane. Peter seemed happy that day. We talked for about ten minutes until they announced his turn to be seen by the doctor. He came off as a pleasant man. I would later find out they sent him to solitary confinement for reasons unknown. One thing I do know is that every chance an inmate got to get him spaghetti, they delivered it.

Every day after the business lunch with J-Lo, I would eat with Lantigua and his bunkie, Rivas. Lantigua was the giant Hispanic guy who loaned me his extra shower shoes. The ones that looked like they fell out of someone's ass. It was a nice gesture nonetheless.

Not long after I moved in in with Steve Yi, the unit manager assigned me a job in the kitchen-the worst job in the unit. Fittingly nicknamed "Water World", since there was a 100% chance you were going back to your unit soaked from head to toe. It was the most uncomfortable feeling working for eight straight hours soaking wet. It was here that I learned how the food was cooked. Its expiration date meant nothing to the powers that be. One day, while stacking large pots and pans for hours on end, a crate of food and fruit was wheeled through the kitchen. On the outside of the box read "Not for human consumption, inmates only". I nearly lost it. What I would have done for a cell-phone camera that day!

You want horror stories? Just google MDC Brooklyn and get ready for some bone-chilling tales. We used to steal oranges, bananas and eggs in the kitchen to satisfy our hunger. I once stole an orange and hid behind the enormous machine used to wash and dry the food trays. I was so excited. I ripped off the top of the orange, and I thought I was seeing things. It looked like a black, hairy tarantula was staring back at me. Luckily it was just mold. That didn't stop me. I ripped off the layer of black mold to where it was just an orange and ate it. That's how desperate I was for fruit. When you're hungry enough, you will eat anything or get used to not eating at all.

For the people in the SHU, their expired food was cooked and reheated twice before consumption. The concrete floor in the kitchen was so slippery that to walk, you had to slide or wipe out and injure yourself. It was mopped with what looked like toilet water at the end of every day by inmates. I have no idea how it passes inspection; it was a complete disaster. I couldn't wait to write this because of the suffering I endured and other inmates are enduring now. I could go on for another hundred pages about this hell hole. We worked through Thanksgiving as if it didn't exist. We ate what looked like turkey only because it still had feathers.

MDC Brooklyn consists of two buildings side by side and connected by an underground tunnel that is used to move prisoners. Working in the kitchen, I would move large vats of food from building to building via the tunnel to inmates in the SHU and our female counterparts. We would always get excited to see the female inmates. It was rare, but I had the luxury of that experience while transporting dinner; it involved a trip on the elevator. After boarding, the CO screams, "Inmates face the wall!" When the warden enters the elevator, shaft inmates must turn away to avoid making eye contact with the boss man. He was a jerk-off. I had a run-in with him later when I got thrown in the hole for a month.

My other job at MDC was cutting hair. I did it for free because most inmates in Brooklyn had nothing to give me. The equipment was atrocious; the clippers were held together with black tape and couldn't cut through butter. The scissors had round balls on the end so they couldn't be used as a weapon. I cut my own hair one day in my cell and thought I had cleaned it all up.

Then, my name was called over the loudspeaker to report to the unit manager. I thought, "Oh, fuck, what did I do?" I went into his office, and he asked me to sit down. He said, "who cuts your hair Martino?" At that moment I knew why I was in his office. I must have left a hair follicle behind and my anal bunkie must have told on me. I said, "I cut my own hair," and he replied , "Good answer, Martino, you were on your way to the hole if you lied." Then he added, "Do it again and I'll clip your wings, Martino. You hear me?" He stood up and shouted again, "I'll clip your fucking wings." There it was, my new bunkie dropped the dime on me. No wonder he had no bunkie; nobody wanted to bunk with this dude, and I was stuck with him, for now!

The next day, a corrections officer approached me to let me know that *I* was wanted in the other unit. The only way to get to the other unit was to be summoned by the wise guys. They had pull in there. They even had spaghetti on some nights. They were friendly and mostly all were wise guys. My unit was made up of Blacks, Hispanics and a sprinkling of Jews. It seemed like there was racial segregation going on, and I was on the wrong side. There were only a handful of white guys in my unit.

One was a leg breaker from Taunton, Massachusetts named Larry Crites. I called him Critesy. Anyway, in the other unit, I was approached by Battista, who was concerned that I was dining with the gays. He was genuinely troubled that I was getting a reputation. I tried to tell him that I've been eating with Lantigua and Rivas, the manliest of men, or so I thought. "Larry will be looking for you tomorrow after work. Hang with him", he said in his most fatherly voice. The next day, I was sitting at a lunch bench in the common area when this hulk of a man lumbered down the center of the community room. He was looking for me.

Larry was six-feet six-inches tall and 260 pounds, and he was about to become my lifelong friend. Larry sat down and nicely said, with a strong Boston accent, "Tommy, you're hanging with the fags. You gotta knock that shit off!" So, from that day on, I ate lunch with Larry. That night, Lantigua shouted from the upper tier, "What's the matter? We're no good for you?" What the hell is going on around here. I thought doing time was supposed to be a break from society's ill wills. Prison is only a microcosm of the outside. Two days later, Lantigua asked me to cut his hair in his room. I obliged. Even if he were gay, I wasn't about to ignore him because of his sexuality.

In MDC Brooklyn, inmates had a ritual of making an incision in their penis with a razor blade and inserting a domino that had been shaved down to the size of a ball bearing. The goal was to allow it to heal and become a permanent fixture in the foreskin. Lantigua informed me that it was a gift for the wives upon their return home. It heightened the sexual experience. I saw them huddling in a room and coming out with bloody towels one night and thought, "Some wife is going to be happy when that dude gets home."

All day, Lantigua reminded me about his haircut. I tried to ignore him but knew eventually that I'd have to shit or get off the pot. The day of reckoning came. He waved me up from the top tier. It was the first time I was ever in his room. It was amazing how some inmates got preferential treatment. Seems like the longer your sentence, the better off you were.

Lantigua's and Rivas's room was like a bachelor pad. They had posters hanging from the top bunk, and it was a mess. And here I was getting in trouble for leaving a hair in the sink. They even gave me shit if I didn't make my bed right. Hell, Lantigua's hadn't made his bed in a week, and he had everything I needed to cut his hair-clippers and all: good clippers to boot. He wanted me to use scissors on top though. Probably so the haircutting process would take longer. I was trying to fly through it, so I could roll out of there.

He started talking about the dominos, and I was freaking out inside. When I finished his cut, he stood up and said, "Tommy, don't forget, if you ever want this let me know, and he pulled out his dick. It was enormous and had around five domino balls implanted under his skin. I was horrified and said, "Okay. I'll let you know." I took off like a bat out of hell. I couldn't believe my eyes. Critesy was right. Lantigua and Rivas were on the down low, and Lantigua wanted me from day one when he offered me the shower shoes. Thank God for Critesy! My bodyguard, pictured on the next page-at my wedding.

We stayed up at night and talked for hours. We played spades, which is a card game played by inmates to pass the time. Critesy was the best company to have in jail, and nobody bothered me. If they did, they would pay a hefty price. Things were getting hairy with my new bunkie-another weirdo freaked out on me one night for farting through the mattress. What was I supposed to do? Save it for a rainy day? He reminded me of an old girlfriend, nagging, unhappy, and miserable. So, I put in for a transfer from his room and found out later that I was the fifth bunkie to remove themselves from his company.

I told the inmate responsible for cell placement that I was moving in with fellow inmate, Bo, to get away from Yi. I pleaded with him to keep it between him and me. It cost me five cans of tuna fish, but it was worth every gill. Within minutes Yi knew of my plan and freaked out. Evidently, the tuna wasn't enough. Days before this, Yi asked me about Battista. I made a crucial mistake and told Yi that if it weren't for Babba, I wouldn't have been in this mess. Once Yi found out about the move, he ran back and told the wise guys and Babba what I had said to get revenge.

Battista, in defense of himself, started a rumor that I was a snitch. He based his tall tale on the week I spent in Brooklyn protecting my mother from testifying. He was also saving his hide. I understood his motivation. It was every man for himself in there- like a bad soap opera. I'll take the blame; I shouldn't have said that to Yi. My bad, Babba.

What happened next almost killed me. I called my attorney and requested my judgment and committal papers to prove I wasn't a snitch or informant. I told her that I was in trouble and that Battista was spreading rumors. I needed those papers or life would be hell for the remainder of my stay. Little did I know the warden was listening. It's a known fact that at MDC Brooklyn they listen to all phone conversations and read all the mail, and then reseal the envelopes. Whenever I got mail, it was clear that it had been opened and scotch-taped shut.

The following day, out of nowhere, Critesy got shipped off to Otisville Correctional Facility. Two hours later, while I was sulking in my room, they locked down the unit. Last time they did that, they found a shank in an inmate's mattress. This time, they were coming for me.

First came the announcement from the corrections officer, "Everybody, retreat to your cells!" I didn't know what to think, but I didn't think they were coming for me, that's for sure. Once they made the announcement, you could hear simultaneous clanging of cell doors slamming shut. Boom! In came a group of officers on a mission. They headed straight for the stairs beneath my cell. I was on the top tier for the first time in this unit, and things were awesome with Bo-even if it was my first day as his bunkie. He was a cool dude, man. It would have been nice finishing out my sentence with him. But they had other plans for me.

I saw the officers using a key to open my cell, then telling me to back away. Rivas had sold me a watch that his wife had smuggled in during her latest visit. They were there to confiscate the watch; I was cooked! They handcuffed me and took me straight to the hole. Once there, they put me in a stand-alone cell. I felt like a gorilla being transported to another zoo. It was a small, four-sided cell, not even enough room to lay down. They made me strip down to my birthday suit for what felt like hours. I was cold and naked as employees walked by to get a glance at the freak show. It was humiliating to say the least.

They finally gave me clothes; it was that same damn oversized stinky-ass orange jumpsuit. Throw in a pair of stiff, yellow underwear and the ensemble was complete. I was going back to hell. The only difference? That hell was exponential! I entered the hole on December 9th at 175 pounds and would leave one month later on January 9th at a mere 127 pounds. They tortured me both mentally and psychologically; they attempted to steal my soul. I was held captive for exactly one month. It's the maximum they could legally keep you while they investigate why you're actually there. The only thing I knew was that they wanted to teach me a lesson. They interviewed me to get my side of the story and said they would get back to me. They never did. What happened to me in that month was disturbing, and some things I saw were astounding. Inmates celebrated at midnight on Christmas and New Years as if they were in their living rooms with a cold beverage in hand- banging on the cell doors for hours screaming and celebrating. It's a good thing prison officials didn't hand out hats and horns. Every morning, I awoke before sunrise to a monotone, spine-chilling Muslim chant with calls of prayer to Fajr. It was a way to acknowledge and remember God. Someone I needed very badly!

At first, I thought it was the Taliban. Maybe it was. After all, I was in the hole, and they have an affinity for caves. Every time I hear that chant, it takes me back to the SHU. It was a tiny, little cell with a rectangular opening in the door where they slid the inedible food. The mirror above the sink was scratched so that you couldn't see yourself. There was one window facing Liberty Island where the Statue of Liberty proudly guards the city of New York. This window intentionally fogged up so you couldn't see her. An inmate once told me a jailhouse secret. The only way to see out was to get jelly and water, mix it together and wipe it on the window. I did it, and it worked temporarily-maybe for a minute or two. It was a treat to see Lady Liberty- a symbol of hope-so whenever I got my hands-on jelly, I would stalk her from a distance.

The shower was tiny and made of metal and it never got a chance to heat up. It sprayed just enough to get you wet, and then it would turn off, leaving you standing there in the cold. Then you'd have to push the button again for another ten seconds. If you wanted more, you had to keep pressing. And to make matters worse, it had a musty smell that only unfinished basements can appreciate; It was brutal. I must have only taken one shower in that month I was there. Think about taking a cold shower outside in December-that's what it was like. I had no choice as my balls were bleeding and sore. It wasn't my balls exactly; it was where they linked to the inside of my legs; they were so sore and raw.

Also, the detergent they used was so pungent and strong that the clothes irritated your skin. The rash was a result of this combination. It took a lot of thought and nerve to jump back into that shower but I had no choice. It sucked but felt good on my balls, and I was glad it was over.

My sink and toilet were metal also. Both were full of stagnant water with what looked like blood clots floating on top. I asked the CO to please fix it, and he said, "The whole floor is like that. Deal with it!" Liar! They moved me every week, and my next cell sink wasn't clogged. It was torture. It took me four days to get a toothbrush!

How could I brush my teeth anyway? The sink would overflow. I brushed them in the cold shower instead, which took about a half-hour. I didn't care. Remember, all you had was time. The more you could kill with an activity, the better.

The floor was full of orange dust bunnies from the toxic clothes we had to wear. Once a week, they would pass a disgusting, dirty-ass, broom bottom through the food door. We were expected to sweep our own floors from our knees. Cinderella had nothing on me. The same broom bottom was used for years on every room. The floors were cleaner than that broom; it had dust bunnies all tangled inside. We all know how bunnies reproduce so imagine the amount of dust I had to inhale-fucking disgusting living conditions.

They had a red emergency button to push in case of an emergency. However, there were consequences if pushed. Nothing was an emergency to these people. That place was run by overpaid, lazy hoodlums who didn't give a shit about inmates and who had no interest in their job performance. The bums running the joint were bigger criminals than the ones in their care. On this one particular day, the inmate in the cell next to mine flew into a rage. He flooded his cell by stuffing a roll of toilet paper into the hole of the cesspool. Continuously flushing will create a river of excrement that's uninhabitable. He also made sure he shit and pissed in the toilet first. I know this first hand because the water seeped through to my room. It was disgusting, and they let him do it. He hit that red button fifty times, and no one did a damn thing. I hit it once for a toothbrush, and I was told I risked finishing my sentence there.

The food was an abomination. Working In the kitchen allowed for a front-row view of the food that went to the SHU. The food, which was past the expiration date, was reheated twice before consumption.

I remember getting French fries one day, and as I attempted to pull one up from the tray, the whole bunch lifted at once; it was one huge French fry! As hungry as I was, I couldn't eat it. I couldn't eat any-thing. Breakfast was the only exception. Some mornings, I didn't even get breakfast. They would give two to a select few. It was a small pint of whole milk-similar to snack time in kindergarten. A Dixie cup filled with cocoa puffs accompanied the milk. That's what I lived on in the hole for a month: milk and cocoa puffs. I learned that being hungry was a normal occurrence. I adapted very quickly.

I made a calendar from loose-leaf paper I finally received a week into the SHU experience. It was a beautiful calendar of December and January. This way, I knew what day it was. Every evening, when the sun went down, I knew it was five o'clock, and the highlight of my day was crossing off the present day; I couldn't wait to do it. There was no other way of telling the time. I couldn't even switch my light on or off. The light switch was outside the cell controlled by the hoodlums. They were torturing me in there.

I once asked for a book, so they put the bookcase right in front of my cell, out of arm's reach. Critesy and I used to spend hours talking to the one CO who had a heart. His name was Ken. He once told me that he treated the inmates with respect out of fear of seeing one of us "on the outside". He also told us of a transsexual who got thrown in the hole the day before for giving blow jobs in exchange for commis-sary. Underneath her bunk was more commissary than the jailhouse bookmaker. Incidentally, the jailhouse bookmaker was Battista.

I yelled to Ken from my cell, and he said, "Dude, what the fuck are you doing in here?" I said, "Can I please have a book?" He handed me three. I devoured them in less than a day. I remember the books were so bad pages were missing. The last book I read had the final two chapters missing. You know what they say, you're never alone if you have a book to read. I kept asking for the warden. I wanted to go back to general population. I felt like I was dying a slow death in there.

Ken let me know that the warden only visits the hole once a week. A week later, there he was. He approached my cell door. With a smirk, his lips were able to verbalize the following sarcastic retort, "Why are you stressing, Martino?" I started to explain, and he abruptly cut me off saying, "Martino, I know more about you than you do," and walked away.

I realized then that I had to change the way I was thinking. I had to chill out and relax and take each day as it came. I had to compartmentalize-something I used to criticize my ex-girlfriend for mastering. At least, I had a canvas from which to copy. I mastered it and barely survived each day. One inmate wasn't so lucky. A guard summoned a gurney for a guy who had been dead for over eight hours. As I said, the normal smell was so repulsive that a corpse would somehow spruce things up. The guards got a slap on the wrist and started an occasional flashlight check to avoid a repeat performance. They'd peer in and say, "Hey, you still alive?"

When the warden came by the following week, I decided to prepare myself. I got up on the top bunk, crossed my legs and opened a book I had finished the day before. I acted like I was on the beach, getting a tan, in Key West, Florida. He peaked in my window. I waved, and he went about his business. I knew it pissed him off. They liked it when you acted desperate. I wasn't going to play into his hands. I wanted him to think that he wasn't affecting me. I created a stir about being called a snitch, so he threw me in the hole as alleged protection as if I were better off in the hole. I got thrown in there because I opened my mouth. He shut it. It felt like I was in the zoo and he was the zoo keeper.

It was Christmas Eve. At midnight, all the inmates went nuts celebrating, laying on the ground, kicking the doors for hours; I thought it would never stop. It was maddening on so many levels. Number one, what the hell were they celebrating for? Number two, I wanted to go to sleep and be done with that holiday. The next day was Christmas. Like a dumb ass I thought, maybe that day we would get something edible to eat like turkey. It wasn't turkey at all; it was pepper steak. I would've rather eaten a rubber band. It was all fat and chewy. I tried to eat it but ended up spitting it out. I sat on my cot for hours staring at the tray of food; I had nothing else to do. Suddenly, a fly joined me; it had made it through my vent and was making that familiar buzzing noise. It was so loud, it almost sounded like he was pissed. I was hoping he was hungry.

If nothing else, I could at least feed the fly. I was watching its every move. I even gave it a name. Miguel, the Spanish Fly! Then the dumb bastard landed on my steak. That fly was in for a world of shit. It's tongue came out and tasted the steak. It was nice to see that the slop would get eaten. It might as well have been a maggot with wings or, even better, one with a badge. What happened next was something for the ages. The fly took off after just a taste. I watched it fly back towards the vent and disappear. I wanted to follow it. It made perfect sense; the food was so terrible even the fly couldn't stand it. It obviously left to find a pile of shit somewhere. That pepper steak wasn't suitable for a fly let alone Christmas dinner.

It was so cold in that room that it was hard to sleep. The guards gave us one sheet and one thin blanket, if that's what they want to call it, one pair of socks and one pancake pillow, probably filled with microscopic animals. One of everything so we couldn't build a noose. They wanted to kill us. They didn't want us to kill ourselves. My hair was falling out, and my muscles had atrophied. My ass bone was so sore I had to sleep on my side. It was getting to that point (where my health was in jeopardy, and I need to get out of there.

I had a visitor – it was my dad and brother. The female CO made me back into the food door and stuck both wrists through so she could cuff me. I was so emaciated that if I wanted to, I could have slid my wrists through the cuffs. Where the hell could I go? She said, "Honey, you better start eating." "Eat what?" I asked her. She didn't respond. I couldn't even force that shit down my throat. Before she took me to my visitors, I shaved really quick but couldn't see myself. Then she led me out into a bigger gorilla cage. My dad and brother were sitting there; they were silent-prisoners themselves for what they witnessed getting to the SHU, I'm sure. I hadn't seen them in months.

When they looked at me, I could tell they were hiding how they felt. My dad's eyes welled up for the first time ever. He said, "Tom, what happened to your face? It's all cut up." I hadn't seen myself for a month, so I had no idea what he was talking about. My face was torn from the shave but I had no way of knowing that, and I was down to 130 pounds from 175; I lost 45 pounds in one month from starvation. I was dying in there, slowly but surely. My dad told me how he had money saved up for me when I got out to help get me back on my feet; It made me feel better, which was his intention. Then they asked to see my stomach. My ribs protruded through the skin and I could tell that they were shocked to see me in that condition by the look on their faces.

In the cell next to us was a drug-cartel inmate with scars all over his face. His attorney was shuffling through documents. We waved at each other and smiled. I'm not exaggerating nor am I a martyr; I'm telling it like it was. You were a number in there, and my number was 75379053. I forgot my number over the years but went back to my notes that I wrote in the clink; I call them my *jail diaries*.

I would jot down notes and send them home to my Mom.

Whenever they changed our cells in the hole, they would first put us outside in a cage to wait while they prepared our new home. I remember seeing a plane fly by and thought, "I can't wait!" I realized the hole must be on the top floor of the building once I saw the roof-top cages. You never know where you are at any given time because the buildings are so creepy. On the ground were filthy jackets you had to put on in order not to freeze.

One morning, exactly thirty days later, around 3:15 a.m., I was awakened by the sweet sounds of jingling keys. Were they coming for me? I heard, "Martino, gather your belongings. You got fifteen minutes." What the hell belongings are they talking about? I didn't have anything. I was beyond excited. I took my calendar, folded it and tucked it in my pocket. I waited on the cot until they returned. The CO came back and led me to the garage where a greyhound bus sat running, with smoke coming from the exhaust. All I wanted to do was get on that bus, get warm and get the fuck out of MDC Brooklyn.

The CO at the garage asked to see my picture ID. He looked at the ID, looked down at me, did a double take and asked if I was okay. That was the first sign of compassion from an employee since my arrival. I couldn't see myself, so I didn't know how I looked. He summoned another co-worker and asked him to look at the same ID. Baffled looks led to the inevitable question, "Is this really you?" I nodded yes and pleaded with them, "Get me the fuck out of here! Still unsure of my identity, they requested my original file.

Soon, they were able to verify my tattoo and that was my ticket onto the bus. They handed me a peanut butter and jelly sandwich and shackled my hands and feet to the bottom of the bus . I wanted to sleep, but it was tough to lie down with the shackles. I managed to, at least, rest my head on the seat during the drive. We drove toward Boston with stops designed to transport passengers to various prisons. Not all of us were headed to the same destination. I was praying I would be taken to an actual camp.

The bus ride lasted a couple hours with a stop at Dunkin Donuts, so the bus driver and the CO could get a coffee. After all, it was around four a.m. and who knows how far he had travelled already. It was so comfortable on the bus-nice and warm with as much heat as I wanted. I was defrosting; I had icicles hanging from my nuts. I did somehow manage to fall asleep here and there for an hour or two.

I remember seeing snow when we hit Boston. I love Boston! The people remind me of Philly. It's clean but, most importantly, one of my best buddies lives there, Peter Legor.

"Never to suffer would never to have been blessed."
Edgar Allen Poe

CHAPTER 10

Fort Devens
The Prison with a Heart

Once we arrived in Devens, I opened my eyes, and the first thing I saw was this creepy-ass dude staring at me. It was a prisoner sitting diagonally from me. He continued to eyeball me with a predatory look; I stared right back. He methodically turned his head away like the second hand on a Rolex watch. It was a slow, sweeping steady motion-like he didn't want to stop. He had that pedophile look about him. Maybe I didn't look as bad after all. His killer eyes were dilated and dagger-like. Thank the Lord they shackled us to the bus in MDC Brooklyn. For the first time, I felt indebted to them. I prayed he wasn't getting off in Boston. He stayed shackled to the bus as I was unlocked and led off. That was a close one.

I thought I had arrived at Devens when I saw the intimidating high fences with large, circular barbed wire but in fact it was the medical building next door to the camp, which was a real, minimum-security federal camp. There was snow all over. We headed into a holding barracks in single file where it was warm for a change. And nobody was there to make sure we didn't escape. I was shocked coming from such a high-security prison. I couldn't believe it.

This one particular inmate from the District of Columbia told me that when we had been on the bus, the inmates were pissed because I had been holding them up and they were in a hurry to get the hell out of Brooklyn. He also said that when I did finally get on, he thought I had AIDS. I nicknamed him DC. He turned out to be a royal pain in the ass. I should have named him moocher. I felt bad for him because he didn't have much of anything and, believe me, he made sure I knew. No one from his family would add money to his commissary, and the inmates couldn't stand him. He asked everyone for everything, especially me.

The thing was, at Devens, the food was good, very good actually. I mean, I would pay money outside of jail for the food they served. After we checked in at Devens, this sweet woman behind the counter said, "Okay, Thomas, go out those doors, walk across that field and into the main entry." I looked out the window, and said to her, "Walk across that field there? With all the snow, walk out those doors?" She said, "Yes sir!" Still baffled, I replied, "With who?" She laughed and said, "All by yourself, Thomas. You're a big boy."

I couldn't believe my ears. She instructed me to walk to the camp, by myself, outside! I felt like I had PTSD from Brooklyn; we were always on guard. Hesitantly, I opened the door and smelled the fresh air of Boston. The ground was slushy outside. The field had about two feet of snow covering it. You couldn't see the camp from where I stood.

So after, with a quick glance back at the woman, I headed for the hill. I learned later that if you try to escape, they add ten years to your sentence. I can't explain the feeling that came over me. The hill was a beautiful sight. The snow was perfect and bright I had to squint to see what was ahead. There were no footprints; however, my size sevens were about to make their mark. The snow on top had an icy crust to it. Each step sounded like milk being poured onto a morning bowl of Rice Krispies.

It took me about half an hour to get to the camp. If they predicted fourteen inches of snow in Boston, you would either get fourteen or two feet but never less. The snow was there all winter. Not like home where the weathermen would predict a foot and you would get a dusting. Shown on the next page are the doors I walked through, minus the snow. My buddy, Peter, took this picture and sent it to me, so I could put it in my book. Peter's the man! When I walked in the door, I was greeted by laughter and good spirits. One inmate yelled, "Yo, look who's here! It's Ray Liotta."

All my life people have commented on my likeness to Ray, especially when I lose weight. I was finally in a camp where I should have been in the first place. It was a one-story army barrack with high ceilings, cubicles and bunk beds in each, like a rancher's home. It had an ample living space to watch TV, a clean cafeteria with outdoor seating and even a barber shop existed on campus. I could now hone my craft! I quickly borrowed a piece of paper, a stamp and an envelope from this guy, Mike Amato, who was very generous. I wrote a letter to my father. Then I looked around with my letter in hand for a uniformed guard.

I asked myself, "How the hell do I mail this?" A finger pointed to an unlocked door with the instructions, "Go outside. That's where the mailbox is." Again, I couldn't believe my ears. Outside? I walked out the door gingerly to mail the letter as I was still unsure if I'd get reprimanded. The minute I walked out, snowflakes fell from the sky, each one kissing me on my face as if God were directing them toward me. I couldn't hold back my emotions. I was overcome with joy and relief. My prayers had been answered. I went from hell to heaven.

The next six months I added eighteen pounds of muscle, increasing my weight to 145 pounds. This place was amazing compared to Brooklyn. I was about to get a lesson on the proper way to shit in jail. Even the bathrooms were nice. They were stalls, like the ones you've probably seen in restaurants, side by side. There were plenty. The best part was no one could watch and jerk off while you were shitting like at MDC Brooklyn. To go from Brooklyn where everyone knew your business to Devens where you could finally have some privacy was a blessing.

While at JPMorgan, I would save shits until I got to work, so I could get paid while doing so. Devens had high-capacity toilets too. You'd flush once, and even elephant shit would go down the drain. There was no waiting between flushes. You could flush as many times as you needed to and the toilet wouldn't skip a beat.

It was in Devens where I quickly learned the hard way of the now-famous jailhouse flush. I sat to take my first doo doo at Fort Devens and immediately got reminded of where I was. Someone yelled, "Yo! Who the fuck is next to me? Flush the fucking toilet you slob!" I quickly flushed and noticed a constant swooshing noise in the bathroom-flush after flush after flush. Continual flushing! I started flushing away. It was beautiful except for the tiny splashes of water against my ass. It was genius, and I use it to this day and educate people on it. It actually cleans the toilet for you too. Now I flush way before I even sit down.

I learned a lot in jail. I learned how to boil eggs in a microwave without the eggs ever touching the electromagnetic radiation. I learned how to play Spades and cut hair. You, for sure, don't learn those things in cosmetology school. I learned how to compartmentalize and survive under the worst conditions. I even learned to be friends with people I didn't like. It was hard to find a dickhead in Devens, but as fate would have it, I unearthed one.

Meet Kenny. He would tell anyone with ears that I was a snitch because I got twelve months and a day. (That extra day was a gift from the judge for helping them tie up loose ends in the case and gave me time off my sentence.) But it sucked because it made me a target. I might as well have had the scarlet "S" sewn on my jumpsuit.

Kenny wouldn't even look in my direction. Not that I gave a fuck, but I'm the type of guy who doesn't take shit from anyone. I don't care if the guy is bigger than me, tougher than me, or stronger than me, I would never back down from anyone. I don't mean Kenny, because he wouldn't last two seconds against me. He was in his seventies but he looked eighty-five. Talking out of his ass was what pissed me off. Grumpy old fuck. Inmates would tell me the things he'd say. For some reason, he didn't like me even though we had never been formally introduced.

I had calluses from walking so much. At Devens, you could go outside during the day for hours at a time. There was a softball field and a basketball court. Both were surrounded by a track for walking. I once spent hours around that track-just me and my thoughts. Every day, I walked, and when the summer months approached, I even sunbathed.

But I knew Kenny was a neat freak so just to irritate him, I shaved my calluses off the bottom of my feet, clipped my toenails and delicately placed them in a pile. During his daily run, I threw the callused shavings and toenails onto his perfectly manicured bed. I even strategically placed some on and under his pillow thinking, " Take that you crabby bastard; revenge is sweet."

The unit manager knew I was coming. He knew my entire situation-even the hole. He was a cool dude and did a great job running Devens. Realizing I was physically in bad shape, he assigned me the best job at the camp, cleaning the gym, which included a weight room where the officers would work out.. It was connected to the kitchen and an auditorium where the CO's hosted events, and I lucked out; I got there in time to see their Christmas tree with my soon-to-be buddy, Johnny Deprospo or it would have been my first Christmas without one. Johnny was a weightlifter who helped me gain back muscle.

To get to the weight room, we had to walk about ten minutes, which was was another nice luxury considering we had twenty-four-hour lock down at Brooklyn. One day, while we were walking to the weight room, we saw a flock of wild turkeys. On another occasion, we saw a coyote. Every day, a mockingbird would show up and mimic the songs of the other birds, often loudly and in rapid succession; these sightings were a treat.

To gain muscle, I would sneak milk from the kitchen for extra protein every morning. I wouldn't necessarily sneak it. I had it delivered by my buddy, Danny Ortega, who worked in the kitchen in the morning. I would wake to milk and the smell of a breakfast sandwich.

Danny was Spanish as were many of my friends in Devens. My bunkie, John Marrera, pictured on the next page, was another in a long line of Papis who entered my circle of trust. I was starving in that picture. Danny didn't get to use commissary because he had no one to send him money, but he offered me so much in exchange for about thirty bucks of commissary every two weeks so I helped him out: it was a deal I couldn't refuse. Plus, he was a good guy and could use the commissary. Even though the food was excellent at Devens, you still needed commissary for stuff like sneakers, tuna fish, Pepsi, etc. He would get me anything I wanted. If I liked something at dinner, I would get two servings. I had a cooler in my locker and Danny would fill it with ice to chill my milk. He was good company and good people, and man could he cook a mean breakfast sandwich.

The food was so good at Devens. It's funny what some seasoning will do. It's even funnier how good food will taste when the expiration date hasn't been reached. The French fries were beautiful-fresh and crispy. The cheeseburgers were just like Mom made-even the meatloaf was good. I'm not shitting you. Eating outside was also a nice perk. Food is everything in jail.

Two of my best buddies worked in the kitchen, so I had the market cornered. I had a cook in my hip pocket; his name was Eddie Portella. Jail was like Delaware County; it was a fraternity of sorts. Everyone had a connection. It was criminal how much we had in common. Pun intended! For instance, my bodyguard Larry Crites, from Brooklyn, got transferred to Otisville and met a man who was my bunkie in the hole for one day; his name was Isiah Suazo. I would have never remembered his name if not for my jail diaries. Isaiah was HIV positive, and we were cellmates in the hole until he got sent off to a camp.

If you remember, in a previous chapter where I describe why Larry was incarcerated, I mentioned an accomplice named Anthony St. Laurent Sr. Well, the Saint was in the medical center at Fort Devens just down the hill, which brings me to Eddie Portella. He spent time with St. Laurent in the medical center too. According to an article in the Boston Globe, Eddie played a key role in getting the Saint put away for good. Eddie disappeared the day before the article was published.

That morning, I saw Eddie get in an unmarked white car with tinted windows just outside the barracks at Devens. The scuttlebutt was his sentence was revoked in exchange for his help in putting the Saint away. Eddie is now in the Witness Protection Program. I hung out with Eddie every night and had a blast. We used to stay up until 2 a.m. talking about everything from the Saint to Larry Crites to other local bookmakers and handicappers in the Boston and Rhode Island areas. He claimed, at the time, he didn't know Larry but apparently, he did.

I missed Eddie when he was gone. He used to bring me whatever I wanted to eat; He would even surprise me with double-decker cheeseburgers. This would tick off the other inmates. On Friday nights, we cooked in groups using the microwave oven. Each of us had to contribute something, whether it be an onion, which was a prized possession when cooking, a bag of Doritos, tortillas or the piece de resistance...Oodles of Noodles. Inmates would call it "a car". I don't know where that came from, but you would get asked during the day, "Hey, you wanna get in our car tonight?" In other words, break bread.

My car was with the Spanish guys. I didn't hang with the Italians because of old man Kenny, but I'd rather be with the Spaniards. The aces are pictured on the next page. Angel is the one with the necklace. He was one of the toughest guys in camp. Another bad ass was John Larrivee. He kept to himself-never bothered a soul. I have to mention John because, like Larry, he looked after me, and I appreciated it.

I was also a barber in Devens. Today, I'm ten times the cutter I was and can fade(A Fade originated in ethnic barber shops and has become the popular term for an aggressively tight taper in men's hair) with the best hairdressers in Delco. There were two of us cutting hair at Fort Devens. That lasted for about a month. The other hair specialist brushed up against a female unit manager in the kitchen and was sent to the hole for the remainder of his sentence. Apparently, you can't even touch a female employee. He was a bully around camp, and no one was upset he was gone. I know what it's like in the hole, but I didn't have time to feel sorry for anyone.

This was a blessing for me because it gave me the opportunity to hone my craft as I was now the sole barber. As payment for cutting an inmate's hair, I would be presented with the commissary of my choice. I also gave a lot of free cuts. I never asked for anything but, if you could afford it, I wasn't shy about greasing my skids. I always asked for a Pepsi-that was my favorite treat. Generous guys like Mike Amato would give me two. I'd drink one a day and wouldn't gain a pound because of the walking I did.

Inmates would sign up for a cut by putting their names on a chalkboard outside the barber shop. It wasn't just craniums I cut. Eddie Portella asked me to shave his back. I thought, "What the fuck. Why not?" Eddie was a little on the chubby side, which was one of his many endearing qualities. I was shaving Eddie's back with the clippers, and we were laughing our asses off, which made the process even longer. It was so funny because here we were in jail, and I was clipping Eddie's back hair in the middle of the day.

It was at that moment that an inmate we called "Cuz" walked by the barber shop and did a double take. He started cracking up before walking away. This made us laugh even harder. It was one of the funniest moments in jail, and I'll remember it forever.

Eddie and I were buddies, and we bonded that day. Cuz was known throughout the camp as a canary with the unit manager because of his singing ability; personally. I liked him in spite of it! It was evident from the beginning that Cuz's rubber band had snapped a long time ago. Everyone knew Cuz was a stool pigeon, but he had protection outside the barbed wire; no one fucked with him as a result. His brother was a soldier in the New England crime family and Cuz told me he was a stone-cold killer. I had no intention of fucking with Cuz even before I learned of his family connection. We were buddies from the start, and he was good-hearted.

The back-shaving incident was cut short by the intercom, "Thomas Martino, please report to the unit-manager's office". His door was shut, and he was on the phone. He saw me and waved me in anyway; that was the type of guy he was-a former military soldier who cared about the inmates and got to know everyone on a personal basis. He was there to help inmates get back on their feet. The true meaning of rehabilitation. He said, "Martino, please tell me you didn't just shave Portella's back." The first person I thought of was Cuz. Fucking Cuz dropped the dime. The unit manager asked me if I was out of my fucking mind. He reminded me of the penalty for this mishap...the hole.

I saw the hole in Fort Devens, and it was nowhere near as bad as Brooklyn. I still didn't want to go. No fucking way. On a scale from 1 to 10 with 10 the being the worst, Brooklyn was a twelve and Fort Devens was a five. Any solitary confinement was terrible. Even though Cuz was a pain in the ass, and no one would fuck with him, I didn't see him that way. I thought he was a character and loved hanging out with him. Cuz used to razz everyone because he knew he could get away with it.

Inmates would talk all the time about the big plans they had when they got out of jail; it helped comfort them. It was a coping mechanism because anybody that goes to jail knows that when you get out, the deck is stacked against you. You have to work your ass off to get your respectability back. Cuz would walk by my cubicle every day.

He'd stop, look at me with a straight poker face, frown, point right at me and say, "You're gonna do big things when you get out Tommy... big things!" He'd turn away laughing at a decibel level that could be heard all across Boston.

He would mock inmates discussing their future, mostly the phony Italians and an alleged Irish mobster. Cuz knew what it was like to be a real gangster. He grew up with one. The boys across the aisle from us at Fort Devens were faking it. I'm not going to mention names, but it was nauseating. Cuz got out right before I did, and I didn't want to see him go. I was happy as hell for him though. There were a lot of fun things going on at Fort Devens. My brain was still on the rebound from the beating I took in Brooklyn. They even had a basketball tournament out in the recreation area, which was super fun. I got a chance to dust off my rusty basketball skills. I could still compete at a high level. My buddy, Bird, though, owned the title of "King". He was the most talented of us all. We played football, softball, wall ball and horseshoes.

Walking the track was my favorite past time. My good buddy, Fudge, taught me how to protect my scalp from sunburn. I saw him one day with a wet washcloth on the top of his head and so I followed his lead. Fudge was a trip. He would trade me a bag of Doritos for a bag of tortillas any time I wanted, and Doritos were more valuable; he was a good dude. I returned the favor whenever he needed a smoke.

I stood guard while he snuck past the "NO-INMATES-BEYOND THIS-POINT" sign. If someone was coming, I would fake a sneeze to warn him of impending danger. If they caught us, we would have been fucked. I took a puff one day for the hell of it and got whacked out of my brain. It was a nicotine buzz but felt like marijuana, but not as good. We found the cigarettes left behind by the CO's outside the auditorium during one of their ceremonies. I wondered if they left them on purpose so we could catch a buzz.

Fudge got his name from his dark complexion. I loved Fudge, he was one of my favorites. Cigarettes weren't the only thing we found while cleaning the auditorium. One day we stumbled onto a stale chocolate cake with vanilla icing; it was three-quarters eaten. You would have thought it was the last supper when we found it. We were like a pack of starving hyenas in the African interior gobbling it up. I once found a piece of pizza in a trash can still in the box. I ate it as if the delivery boy had just left. Another delicacy was coffee creamer; they would often leave it behind; it was coveted by all inmates-the real deal, straight from Dunkin Donuts, not that powdered shit we were drinking during the day.

I remember the day I found the pizza. Johnny Deprospo and I found a mouse stuck to a mouse trap in the same trash can. The mouse was alive and running for its life but getting nowhere. The little guy was clearly suffering, but neither of us were about to pull him off the sticky substance and get gnawed. It wasn't the conventional mouse trap that snaps their head off. It was the trap with a glue-like substance that attracted rodents. We both agreed, after much deliberation, that we had to put the mouse out of his misery as quickly as possible; he was suffering more than I did in Brooklyn. We went and retrieved a mop, took off the handle and ended the mouse's struggle. He was no longer with us. Those traps should be outlawed.

We worked out in the daytime outside using picnic benches. We would do triceps by putting two together and dip between them. We would lay underneath and simulate bench pressing by lifting up the picnic table. For the stronger guys, I would sit atop the bench and move up and down to make the load heavier or lighter. For pull ups, we found an old tree with a low-hanging branch that worked perfectly. We'd strengthen our legs by squatting that same bench. We did it every day with one of us as lookout. You needed three guys to work out; rotation was a must. We weren't permitted this exercise, but I believe they turned a blind eye.

My friends outnumbered my foes at Fort Devens. Almost everyone was personable. If I didn't get along with someone, I just kept my distance. There was this untrustworthy; guy, Charlie, who people warned me about. I usually followed my own instincts when it came to initial meet-ings. Charlie was in his eighties and at the tail end of a ten-year sentence for tax evasion. He kept to himself from what I could tell until one day early in my stay at Devens. He stopped by my bunk and introduced himself. I guess he caught wind that I was there and wanted to meet me.

There was a lot of hoopla when I arrived at Devens because of the scandal. They saw it unfold on TV like all of America. Devens had an auditorium of sorts with three TVs. One had closed captioning for the Spanish inmates. Another was for the folks who liked movies, and the third was strictly for sports enthusiasts. You needed earphones in order to watch and listen from afar. With three televisions going at once, who could hear what was being said by which TV? They knew all about Donaghy and the scandal. I wasn't surprised when Charlie showed up at my cubicle. I was in his house, so it was normal for him to want to know who he'd be living with for the next six months.

He started by mentioning his alleged ties to organized crime. I guess he thought that we would have something in common if he opened with a mob reference. I was used to it. It seemed like almost every inmate at Devens was an alleged mobster, knew one, or was related to one; Charlie was no exception. I don't remember what his alleged association was, but I think it had something to do with the Irish Mob.

No disrespect to old people, I'm old myself, but Charlie was so old I couldn't tell his nationality. He could have been Irish or he could have been Italian. It's not that he was old at eight-five, it's that Charlie looked older than he was. He had a plethora of medical conditions that he would piss and moan about all day long. I could hear him bitching at 5:30 every morning while I was still trying to sleep. "Fuck this! Fuck that!" he would grumble. He was feeling sorry for himself, and it tugged at my heartstrings.

Charlie had no friends at Fort Devens, but I wasn't about to shun him just because everyone else did. I couldn't understand the population's beef with him. Deep down I think his age had a lot to with it. Some people don't like hanging with the older guys. I didn't give a rat's ass about his age. If you're a genuine person, and I can trust you, you're good in my book.

After the attempted mob linkup, he offered me a banana that he took from his job in the warehouse; bananas were currency inside any prison. They just don't hand them out to inmates. The closest I got to a banana in Brooklyn was the Banana who told me I was in a camp when I first got there. Charlie occasionally smuggled yellow apples, my favorite apple on the planet. I think they are called golden delicious apples. Whoever named them got it right on the money. They are golden, and they are fucking delicious. Charlie giving me his banana was very generous; I felt indebted to him.

I cut up the banana, put it between peanut butter, jelly and two slices of bread. It satisfied every sweet tooth in my mouth. Charlie knew I liked bananas; he brought me one whenever he had the opportunity. He had one every day for himself, but whenever he had an extra he would give it to me. He would come by every day, sit down and bullshit with me. Talking smack about the other inmates was his specialty. My father always told me to be wary of the people who talk out of turn. He said that you can bet your bottom dollar they are talking about you too.

Charlie told me he was going to play poker with a group of inmates and asked if I would be his partner but not to play; I was going to fund the operation and if Charlie happened to win, which was often, we would split the proceeds. Whoever won got to use the commissary of the others who lost. The winnings were close to sixty bucks, and all I had to do was put up fifteen of my commissary dollars for Charlie to play. I didn't want to get involved, but I did it for Charlie. He seemed to come to life on the days leading up to the tournament. I would hear the group cheering as they won each round; this was serious shit.

One night, this guy, Phil, went ape shit over a hand he lost. He went nuts because it knocked him out of contention. It took two hours to calm him down. Charlie came over to my bunk after the match and told me with a smile, "We won, Tommy!" I congratulated him. The following week we got to spend an extra thirty bucks each on the loser's commissary. I told him not to pay me, to keep the winning, but he insisted I take my cut. This became an every-other-week thing. I was thinking that I'd better take the winnings and quit while I was ahead. Who the hell knew if he was a one hit wonder? But what do you know? He won again!

We split the proceeds. Charlie was obviously a ringer.

Now, I had a top poker player in my hip pocket. Everyone knew of the deal Charlie and I had made. People were talking about it constantly because he won three times in a row, and we were up 180 bucks. I knew our luck would run out sooner or later. On the fourth week, Charlie came by my bunk with a sad face to tell me we had lost. Charlie came and used fifteen dollars of my commissary that week and life went on until the next tournament – or so I thought.

Later that evening, after Charlie allegedly used my commissary for the person who won, my friend John passed by my bunk. He said, "I can't believe you guys won again!" I said, "What are you talking about? We finally lost!" I was wrong. John witnessed the victory. I couldn't believe it. Charlie lied to me and told me he lost. What the fuck! I wasn't pissed, I was disappointed. I actually had to laugh a little because it was kind of funny. I never said anything to him about it, but I stopped funding his poker tournament. Unfortunately, the bananas went scarce also. He must have known that I found out. He also sensed my indifference. I was still cordial to him, but I did feel betrayed by the man. The worst part was not being able to satisfy my banana craving.

One night, I snuck over to Charlie's bunk, and there he was snoring away like a hungry, old bear, hibernating for the winter. He had his eyes covered with a sleep mask, so the sun wouldn't wake him up in the morning. I never understood this because Charlie was up way before the sun made its appearance. I looked in his locker and there staring back at me was a beautiful banana. I convinced myself it was mine since he ripped me off with the poker tournament. I lifted the banana, brought it back to my bunk and locked it up.

I was going to eat it when he left for work at the warehouse the next morning. It was only going to be a one-time thing until I heard him ranting and raving at 5:30 in the morning. You had to giggle at his tirade, "Fuck this! Fuck that! Somebody stole my fucking banana." I had to hide my face in my pillow because I was laughing so hard. My bunkie, whose job it was to mop the floors before everyone got up, whispered to me, "Did you steal Charlie's banana? He's fucking pissed." I showed my bunkie the banana, and we died laughing. After that day, Charlie would hide his bananas.

Two days later I overheard him tell his bunkie where he was going to hide it and that the thief would never find it. Little did he know the thief was listening. At two in the morning, I snuck over to Charlie's bunk again. There it was, right next to him under his hat. I quietly removed it and took it back to my bunk where it belonged. I kept doing it for fun and to get a good laugh. Charlie's reaction was priceless. There were only so many places to hide a banana. He had no idea it was me.

Charlie got sick and passed away in the medical center at Fort Devens not long after I got released. He never did get to go home. Dying in jail is a lonely death. Charlie didn't deserve that. I like Charlie to this day and think about him every time I see a banana or eat a peanut butter, jelly and banana sandwich.

Life at Fort Devens wasn't always a bed of roses. We were still someone else's property, still just a number. One cold morning in February, the sixth, to be exact, I was approached by the camp bully, Jimmy. He smacked me on my shoulder very hard in front of everyone. He followed the whack with, "What do you say me and you go in the bathroom right now and go sixty percent and see what happens." All the while squeezing my shoulder to try and intimidate me. I knew he was hoping I'd pussy out. He was calling me out in front of everyone. I knew it would happen eventually. He was best friends with old man, Kenny. I wasn't the least bit afraid of Jimmy, and he knew it. Hell, I wasn't afraid of anyone or anything...except that hole in Brooklyn.

He was picking fights every day with someone. He went after Johnny when we were in line for dinner one night. Jimmy was ten years my junior, and his claim to fame was garnering All-State honors in high-school wrestling. There was no doubt Jimmy was tough but so was I. Jimmy suspected as much but couldn't confirm it. Now ten years is a big gap in age when it comes to fighting, but hell would freeze over before I'd back down. I turned to him and said, "Sounds good to me, Jimmy. I have one condition though. I can't go sixty percent, brother. I can only do 110%! I don't know any other way. I don't even know what you mean by sixty percent." I knew what he was up to; he wanted me to go 60% while he gave it 100% to catch me off guard. But I was ready to whoop his ass. He knew it too!

Someone across the cubicle saw what was happening and said, "Tommy, today's your birthday! Happy birthday my friend! I thanked him. It was Mike Amato, one of the nicest guys in Devens. He was correct; it was my birthday. Jimmy looked at me and said, "Today's your lucky day, Tommy. I'm gonna let you off the hook. Happy Birthday!" I knew what he meant. It was his way of not going into the bathroom and risk losing his championship belt to me. He was hoping I would chicken out like everyone else had. Turns out it was his lucky day. He got to retain his title for another day. That's how we became friends. I didn't back down. I didn't win his belt, but I won his respect. Not that I cared, I'm just letting you know that it didn't matter if I had his respect or not. It was my dignity that went unharmed that day. It was all I had left.

After that day, Jimmy would ask me to walk on his back to crack it for him. I didn't mind; I didn't want any trouble. It was the rope-a-dope again. Invented by Muhammed Ali but perfected by me. I just wanted to get home, and I didn't have time for the bullshit. Believe me, it was all bullshit in here. At least, I was in Fort Devens. God sent me here; I'm sure of it.

Every Sunday, I'd hear over the loudspeaker, "Thomas Martino, you have a visitor." Naps were sometimes interrupted by this recurring announcement. You would think I'd be happy about it, and I was; the only problem was it disrupted a dream of home sweet home. I would roll off the top bunk, throw on my visitor uniform, hit the can, splash water on my face and run it through my hair once or twice to keep it from sticking up. Then I'd walk the corridor to the visitor's area.

He was there like clockwork, my dear friend, Peter Legor. I had many visitors at Fort Devens but none as loyal as Peter. I met Peter when I was twenty-one years old by accident on a golf trip in Myrtle Beach, South Carolina. We hit it off immediately and have remained close friends ever since. He's one of the funniest guys I've ever met and reminds me of myself quite a bit. We are the same age, live in different cities, yet we live similar lives.-Tommy in Philly and Peter in Boston.

I've been lucky enough to have a friend like Pete and our friendship has endured the many miles between us. I will never forget how he sacrificed his football-filled Sundays in New England to come see his delinquent, evil twin from Philly whose life was crumbling beneath his own two feet. He constantly reminded me that I was strong and that I would rebuild my life. Peter was never embarrassed by my incarceration. I was no longer a success in life or a young stud, but Peter saw beyond that. We were, and still are, more like brothers than friends, and he stuck by me when it mattered most. I would share with Peter the jail stories each Sunday as they happened.

One time, as Pete was leaving, one of the correction officers asked me if the Celtics were going to win that night. Since the camp was in Massachusetts, I felt obligated to tell him to take Boston. I didn't even know who they were playing that night, and I didn't want to ask. That's how callous I had become to the NBA. I used to bull-shit them because I wanted them to think I was a good handicapper. Don't forget I was trying to survive in this joint. Giving a corrections officer a winner here and there was not a bad thing. I had a fifty-fifty chance. When he asked about the Celtics, Peter blurted out, "Hey

Mark, (with a Boston accent, replacing the "r" with another "a") he never said he was a good handicapper. He was a great cheater!" We all laughed and recant that story whenever possible.

With two weeks left in my sentence, my judgement and committal papers arrived at Fort Devens. It only took six months for them to get there! How appropriate! Did I expect any different from MDC Brooklyn? The postage read January 9th. I should have been ecstatic to see these papers but all this did was confirm my views of the system. At this point, I just wanted to get home.

The Flyers were playing well, the Phillies had just won the World Series, and I was in fucking limbo. My dog needed me, my family needed me, and I needed them. I was counting down the days. A week later, I received a letter in Devens granting me the right to go to a different camp other than MDC Brooklyn so I would not have had to serve my sentence in the same prison as Battista, and I could have avoided the hell hole that was MDC Brooklyn, but it came way too late, which was par for the course.

Battling this faction was next to impossible. They are their own La Cosa Nostra. So, do yourself a favor, stay out of trouble and out of this system because it will bite your dick off and feed it to the alligators. If you ever have to do Federal time, ask if you can do it in Fort Devens, and for Christ's sake, pray to God you don't have to go to MDC Brooklyn!

"I love a success story, but even more than a success story; I like a dude who fucks his life up and gets his life together again story."
Joe Rogan

CHAPTER 11

Half Way Home

After my release from Fort Devens, I was driven by an inmate to the Boston airport where my Dad and buddy, Spike, were waiting for me with open arms. It was a tearful reunion for all of us. The first thing my Dad asked was "What would you like to eat? Anything you want." I explained to my Dad that I didn't want my first meal out of jail to be airport food, and he understood. I wanted veal parmesan, and unless they had a Martarano's restaurant, like in Atlantic City, I was getting on the plane and getting the hell out of there. But I wasn't going home, I still had to serve my last two months at a half-way house in Kensington, Philadelphia.

Every former inmate, including myself, will tell you they would rather complete their sentence in jail than go to a halfway house. It's kind of goofy how they do it. It's like going from one jail to another, only this one was in the depths of Kensington, which is known for its crime and abundance of drugs, specifically, heroin. I seriously thought I was headed to my brother's hair salon to dye my hair black and get rid of all the new gray, but I had just four hours to get to the halfway house or violate my probation.

I took a chance and stopped at the salon, which was about a half hour from the half-way house. It was my brother Chuck's establishment, Nirvana Hair Gallery, now located on Saxer Avenue in Springfield,

Pennsylvania-one of Delco's finest! When I arrived, there were so many mirrors. I took the selfie pictured below. I dyed my hair and headed straight for the badlands of Kensington. Thank God I got to the halfway house, called Luzerne, within the four-hour window and is was a shit show. I believe it closed down a couple years ago.

That place should never have opened to begin with. It was supposed to be a rehabilitation center. When an inmate got there, he or she could reacclimate themselves to life outside of prison. This place did nothing but slow that process to a screeching halt. As surprised as I was to see the horrific conditions of this establishment, I wasn't surprised at all. It was just another example of how the system had failed. They had mindless rules initiated and enforced by mindless individuals.

I had to sleep with twenty people in one room filled with bunk beds. Everyone was snoring so loud, you couldn't even sleep at night. All my roommates had big plans of what they were going to do when they got out of there and they were asking me for money every day to help them. It was annoying to me because first of all I didn't have the money and second of all I was pissed because it was stupid for me to be there, I should have been sent home to work and I could have been kept under house arrest instead.

CHAPTER 12

The Aftermath
Picking up the Pieces

I finally got out of the halfway house and did what I had planned to do-take my dog, Macie, on a date for a salmon teriyaki dinner , at one of my favorite restaurants . It was our favorite meal together. Only this time, she wasn't getting leftovers. I had permission from the owner to let her sit at the table with me (pictured on the next page). She ate like a queen, and I ate like a king. To this day, when I walk into that restaurant, over ten years later, someone from the staff will recall that hot summer day and ask me if Macie is still alive. They are always happy to hear she is doing well. She now has a sister named Pearl.

While in Fort Devens, I was approached about an offer for a book deal; three publishing houses bid and my cut from the top one was for about $80,000. I almost signed but, at the last minute I refused when I found out that the ghostwriter they assigned to me was hell bent on trying to prove Donaghy fixed games and I didn't want any part of that. Instead, I wrote this book and put the finishing touches on in the same kitchen where Battista, Ruggieri, two FBI agents, plenty of escorts and Donaghy all stood.

If anyone thinks I'm facing the darkest time in my life right now, they'd be wrong. I married my best friend in March of 2014, Ashley Martino, pictured on the next page. It was a breathtaking ceremony on the beach at the Waldorf Astoria in Key West, Florida. We have a three-year-old son named Thomas Francis Martino Jr. I am currently employed at Nirvana Hair Gallery as a cosmetologist and I am still in touch with Battista and Donaghy to this day.

"I shall pass through this world but once.

Any good, therefore, that I can do or any

kindness I can show, let me do it now for

I shall not pass this way again!"

William Penn

Epilogue

I would like to thank you for purchasing this book. I can only hope that you enjoyed reading this narrative as much as I enjoyed writing it because it was therapeutic and gave me closure. I promised myself that I would provide a good role model for my son, and I was determined that he would never repeat the mistakes of his father. I am at total peace with myself.

If you loved the book, be sure to catch the movie, *Inside Game,* starring Scott Wolf (*Party of Five, The Night Shift,* most recently the CW's Nancy Drew series) set for release in November of 2019.

Acknowledgements

I would be remiss if I did not express my appreciation to my family and friends. They were my reason for being during the trying times described in this book.

I owe a special debt of gratitude to my cousin, Paulie Martino, who saw great promise in me. Paul understood the compelling nature of the NBA betting scandal. The simple act of including NBA and betting scandal in the same sentence was sensational. Paul readily sensed the gripping nature of the human conflict involved. This narrative promised to go far beyond a simple chronicle of its details. These acknowledgements gave birth to the production of the movie "Inside Game"'. The making of "Inside Game" evolved over several years and encapsulated not only the account of the scandal, but its genesis, the mob involvement and erosion of human values.

Special thanks to my book coach, Ellen Violette, Director of the film, Randall Batinkoff, Producer, Michael Pierce, and many thanks to Tim Donaghy who has proven to me that the strongest friendships can pick up where they left off.

About The Author

First-time author, Thomas Martino, worked for nineteen years as an IT specialist on Wall Street at JP Morgan before he became entangled in the NBA betting scandal that rocked the basketball world and brought him to his knees.

He currently resides in the Suburbs of Philadelphia, with his loving wife, Ashley and their 3-year-old son Thomas Jr. He currently works as a trained professional in the field of cosmetology, his main focus is on hairstyling and grooming for men.

Thomas is a family man who enjoys spending his time off with loved ones. Through hard work and determination, he has rebuilt his life back to respectability and looks forward to enjoying life from now on!

Download your free private interview:
"Easy Money til It Wasn't Video"
where author, Thomas Martino, shares some of his
observations and insights into the NBA Scandal and
the hard life lessons he learned along the way.

www.insidegamebook.com

Made in the USA
Middletown, DE
21 November 2019

79120500R00085